W9-BXN-609

Andrew L. Bouwhuis
Library
Canisius College

Donated in Memory
of
Rev. B. Gibson Lewis, Jr.

THE EPISTLE TO
THE PHILIPPIANS

THE EPISTLE TO THE PHILIPPIANS

KARL BARTH

John Knox Press
RICHMOND, VIRGINIA

Translated by James W. Leitch from the German
ERKLÄRUNG DES PHILIPPERBRIEFES
(6th edition 1947) Evangelischer Verlag AG Zürich

Published simultaneously in Great Britain by
SCM Press Ltd, London
and in the United States of America by
John Knox Press, Richmond, Virginia

Library of Congress Catalog Card Number: 62-8213

BS
2705
.B2

CANISIUS   GE LIBRARY
BUFFALO, N. Y.

© SCM PRESS LTD 1962
FIRST PUBLISHED IN ENGLISH 1962
PRINTED IN GREAT BRITAIN

CONTENTS

PREFACE

WHAT is offered here is the reproduction of a course of university lectures held in the Winter Semester of 1926-27. Mr Hermann Zeltner of Nürnberg, a divinity student, has helped in important ways with the preparation for the press. The intention was to make the work readable for non-theologians too.

I do not propose to enter here into the dispute concerning 'pneumatic exegesis'. Although, if I am not mistaken, I am one of those who occasioned it, yet this unpleasant catch-word at all events is not of my coining. However, for other reasons, too, I have been unable to bring much interest to bear on the dispute—because so many of the all too copious shots aimed at me, not without caricature, have been wide of the mark, but above all because it appears to me to have unfortunately got bogged down in the sphere of methodological discussions, in which a decision is scarcely to be expected. It can hardly be fruitfully continued except as those who do not indeed entirely reject the concretely proposed aim as such, but would certainly wish to take it up in a different and better way, resolve to provide their own examples of an exposition that takes account of the aim in question, and thus show equally concretely how they conceive of this better way. That I myself—though my intention remains the same—do not bind myself to the procedure earlier employed in the case of the Epistle to the Romans, but am still seeking, is a thing the present work will perhaps make clear at least to some.

Münster in Westphalia   KARL BARTH
September 1927

INTRODUCTION

Paul and Timothy, slaves of Christ Jesus, to all the holy in Christ Jesus who are at Philippi (with their overseers and attendants!), grace be with you and peace from God our Father and the Lord Jesus Christ.

1. **Paul and Timothy** give their names as the writers of this letter. It has often been called the most personal of all the Pauline epistles. But at least that does not prevent Paul's doing here what he does also in the majority of his other letters: he does not introduce himself alone and solely in his own name to those he is addressing, but in the company of one of his younger helpers. The fact that Paul goes on at once in v. 3 to speak in the first person singular, and in 2.19 ff. refers to Timothy in the third person, shows that the point of naming two writers here must not be sought in some kind of co-authorship on Timothy's part. Rather, it is Paul's way of saying that the message and contents of the letter are not a sort of private vision that depends on his, the apostle's, own two eyes. A hero, a genius, a 'religious personality' stands alone; an apostle has others beside him like himself and sets them on his own level. He speaks in an office occupied by *many*. *He* can fall, but his Lord does not fall with him. He has other slaves as well. 'Honour' to Timothy lies in this mention of his name only in so far as he sees him involved with himself in the same ignominy and danger. The mention of his name in particular can have been occasioned here by the fact that Timothy according to Acts 16.1 and 17.4 was probably his companion in the stormy events that accompanied the founding of the Philippian congregation, and according to Acts 19.22 had presumably been among them later as well.

Both of them are **slaves of Christ Jesus.** The omission here of Paul's designation of himself as 'apostle' calls attention (as has often been observed) to the fact that Paul here sees no need to assert outwardly the authority he bears. If his reason for doing so in Rom. 1.1 presumably lies in the nature of that particular letter, whose austere, didactic objectivity was to vouch for the apostolic dignity of its author, then we have to think here of the relationship of extraordinary trust between author and readers, which rendered that designation of himself superfluous. That he none the less intends to claim his authority here also in all its fulness, goes without saying. The very designation *slaves* of Christ Jesus' is a reminder of that authority. It points away from the person of the speaker to the Person of his Lord, in its very sharpness even more explicitly if anything than does the word 'apostle'. The speaker is not a man with rights of his own and he does not act as such. He functions. He belongs to his Lord, and his Lord is responsible for him, his Lord answers for him. The speaker stands in his shadow, but in that shadow he is also secure—against all who might chance to question his authority. He is 'as a genuine slave no other man's slave' (Chrysostom).

The designation of the Philippians as **the holy in Christ Jesus** describes the condition in which they find themselves on the ground of a specific mind and attitude towards them on God's part (not *vice versa*!). The Old Testament concept of holiness already points us in that direction. The addition of 'in Christ Jesus' rules out any reflection on the subjective qualifications or worth of the people concerned. For precisely through Christ Jesus in the circle marked by baptism as his community on earth, their subjectivity, such as it *is*, has had the hand of God laid on it. 'Holy' people are unholy people, who nevertheless as such have been singled out, claimed and requisitioned by God for his control, for his use, for himself who is holy. Their holiness is and remains in Christ Jesus. It is in him that they are holy, it is from this point of view that they are to be addressed as such, in no other respect. The holiness of Christians is enduring and true in him who gives it, and that too *in that* he gives them it, not in that *they* have it. 'Our citizenship is in heaven', as we shall hear in 3.20.

The addition **with the overseers and attendants** has always created interest as one of the oldest testimonies to the presence of offices in the Church. Catholic exegetes have rejoiced in the public appearance of 'bishops', just as Calvin rejoiced in the circumstance that the congregation is mentioned first, and only then, indirectly introduced by 'with', the *antistites*. In view of what is now known about the contemporary usage of the two terms, the passage, however correct Calvin's remark in itself remains, probably will not serve for polemic purposes either in the one sense or in the other. Both *episkopoi*[1] (bishops) and *diakonoi* (deacons) were at that time names for certain officials of the state, of the townships and especially of the religious guilds, in particular such officials as had to do with the collection and management of taxes (*episkopoi*) and with the distribution of gifts, e.g. of sacrificial meat at communal meals (*diakonoi*). If that is the analogy on which the concepts are to be understood here, then we should have to think not of 'spiritual' offices in our sense, not of the leaders of Christian public worship in Philippi as such, but of offices of a predominantly administrative character—whereby the probability that those who filled them had a certain position of authority in the congregation, perhaps also in public worship, need not be questioned—except that, as the plural at once shows, it was certainly not the authority of the later bishops. This mention of them, and the strange 'with', is then no doubt to be explained as a first grateful allusion to the collection taken for the apostle in Philippi, to express his thanks for which (4.10 ff.) is one of the purposes of the letter.[2]

2. The apostolic greeting. We say little here, where much too much could be said. It requires little enough reflection to find in

[1] Chrysostom, incidentally, read *synepiskopois* for *syn episkopois*, i.e. 'the (my) fellow-bishops' for 'with the bishops', which reading would make Paul apply this title indirectly also to himself. On the other hand Chrysostom admits that by these bishops is not yet to be understood the later chief pastoral office of that name, but simply the priests of the Philippian congregation.

[2] Ewald-Wohlenberg combine this conjecture with the *ēdē pote anethalete to hyper emou phronein* of 4.10 as follows: Paul wished this specially friendly mention of them to acquit the bishops, etc., of any possible charge of negligence towards him. The support for this in the few words of 1.1; 4.10 appears to me, however, too weak.

this phrase, which Paul has constructed by taking over and significantly recasting older pagan and Jewish formulas of greeting, a compact expression of his whole message. That which on the divine side is so completely the Christians' present and proper possession that it can be *ascribed* to 'all' (v. 1) without more ado, yet on the other hand is also so completely beyond their human possession and keeping that it must be *desired* for them *in prayer*—that which is thus, as the object of common thanksgiving and common longing, the tie that binds the apostle and his congregations[1]—the first thing of which it is appropriate for him to remind them, since it is also the last and the whole, is: **grace and peace.** *Grace*: the merciful 'Nevertheless!' with which God steps out from the mystery of his majesty and holiness and turns to address man, the *ratio* (the point) of his covenant with his fallen and lost creation. *Peace*: the same merciful 'Nevertheless!' with which God, in realization of this covenant, enters into the life and existence of man in order there (but 'surpassing all understanding', 4.7!) to exercise his law and his power. Both are **from God our Father,** in whom we have our distant home and feel the absence of it, **and**—and indeed there is no other God!—**from our Lord Jesus Christ,** in whom our *home* comes *to us* (in whom we here and now already call God 'our Father') in order that *we* may come *home*.

[1] For this characteristic compare the following section, vv. 3-11.

I for my part thank our Lord in all my thoughts of you, always, in all my prayers praying joyfully for you all because of your participation in the Gospel from the first day until now, putting my confidence in this, that he who has begun the good work among you will complete it until the day of Christ Jesus. It is indeed only right and proper of me to think this of you all, because I bear you in my heart as those who in my imprisonment, as also in my defence and declaration of the Gospel, are all my copartners in grace. For God is my witness how greatly I long for you all with the affection of Christ Jesus. And my prayer is: that your love may increase more and more in knowledge and all-round discernment to distinguish what really matters, so that you may be pure and faultless against the day of Christ, filled with fruits of the righteousness which is (created) **through Jesus Christ, to the glory and praise of God.**

3-4. The translation **I for my part thank our Lord** rests on the assumption that the Western text is primary: *egō men eucharistō tō kyriō hēmōn*, which has the advantage of at once leading very concretely to the heart of the matter. Paul knows[1] that the Philippians think of him with anxiety, worrying about him and his fate and his future,[2] and in that vein also praying for him. I for my part, he replies, as if engaged in the midst of a conversation with them—I *thank our common Lord*, when *I* think of *you* and pray for *you*. This insertion[3] has such an original flavour that it seems hardly feasible to take it as a copyist's invention.

Paul **gives thanks.** He has the delicacy not to write something like, 'I give thanks for what you sigh over, namely, my sufferings

---

[1] Only on this hypothesis is the section 1.12-26 intelligible.

[2] It is hard to imagine how it can occur to anyone (Ewald-Wohlenberg) that the Philippians were worried in case Paul were not thanking God.

[3] I.e. *egō men* (I for my part) inserted in the Western text (*Translator*).

for Jesus' sake'—although v. 7 (*charis*, grace) and vv. 19 ff. show
he could also say that—but, 'I give thanks concerning *you*, **in all
my thoughts of you,**[1] as you in your thoughts of me and your
prayers for me are anxious'. I, however, *give thanks*. A gentle
admonition to the readers. The proper basis for thinking of each
other and praying for each other among Christians is, that they
thank their common Lord. That is indeed the proof of whether in
the *prayers* they offer they are really turning to him, the Lord, and
not to some God of their own making. But the sentence is after
all only in *form* a preliminary answer to their expressions of
apprehension. Paul wishes to tell his readers that he rejoices over
them. Not in order to give them something pleasant to hear, but
because he would have them know (and take encouragement and
warning from the knowledge) that when the apostle thinks of
them he praises God. Notice the constant repetition here and in
the following verses of the word 'all'.[2] It is as if they were meant
to see him: the *whole* man concerning himself with them *all*. But
the very fact of this *whole* concern with *all* of them at once lifts
the relationship between him and them beyond any ordinary one
of attachment, recognition and gratitude. 'It is over lost sinners
that God's Spirit is uttering this prayer of thanksgiving, and only
over them' (Horn). It is a question of *God* and *his* work among
men, which one can praise only *in prayer*, in face of the *abysmal
depths* of *everything* human. The Philippians have given him
occasion for that. That is why it is no exaggeration when Paul
says he *thanks* the Lord in *all* his thoughts of them. To the extent
that men are concerned with *God*, their thoughts *about each other*
obviously acquire, despite all the depths of human nature, *one
simple* denominator.

The expression Paul uses is incidentally far stronger than our
translation 'thoughts of you'. *Mneia* is (Rom. 1.9) a readiness to
serve someone, to take his part. That holds here also, as the sequel
shows: **always, in all my prayers for you all.** Considering

[1] Ewald-Wohlenberg take *mneia hymōn* as subjective genitive, so making
Paul give thanks *for the thoughts* his readers *have* (towards him). The weight
particularly of the parallel Rom. 1.9 prevents my following them.
[2] V. 3 *pasē*, v. 4 *pantote, pasē, pantōn*, v. 7 *pantōn, pantas*, v. 8 *pantas*.

men and all things human, no thoughts and no thanks are here
possible except as an act of solidarity and hence supplication,
prayer, intercession. The judgment under which the Philippians
stand in common with all flesh, and as the 'holy' more than all
flesh, is not forgotten. The '*for* you' (*hyper hymōn*) of intercession
for each other presupposes that the man for whom the prayer is
made is *totally* destitute. God must act *for* him, *therefore* I must
pray *for* him. 'God's people live from hunger and thirst after
righteousness' (Horn). That holds also and above all in the fellowship of prayer. Nowhere and never do they live from the riches
discovered in themselves and others. 'Not as if I had already
apprehended or had already reached the goal, but I race on in the
hope that I may apprehend, seeing that I am apprehended by
Christ Jesus', Paul will say later (3.12) of himself by way of
example. He sees the Philippians also 'racing on' under the same
motto: 'Not yet—But!' *Hence* they give him occasion for thanks
and supplication—hence too, however, the supplication is
praying joyfully.

Here for the first time the word 'joy', so characteristic of our
epistle. The context in which it appears should not be overlooked:
meta charas tēn deēsin poioumenos (joyfully praying = expressing
want) is, when we think of the basic meaning of *deēsis = exigentia*,
want, a paradox no less stringent than Luther's *desperatio fiducialis*
(confident despair). It is *this* joy that is the often admired 'joy' of
Philippians. But it is joy. Joy from him and in him to whom Paul
gives thanks, to whom his intercession is addressed, joy from and
in his Self-attestation over all human depths, joy from and in the
Mercy which Paul sees reigning like a triumphant monarch in the
Philippian congregation. For the rest joy from and in—nothing.
Else it would not be the *jubilant* joy which is undoubtedly to be
heard here. Cf. v. 6!

5. The above is not to dispute that the *cause* of the apostle's
thanksgiving was a *concrete* one. Paul indicates his reason with the
words: **because of your participation in the Gospel from the
first day until now.** *Koinōnia* (participation) in conjunction with
'until now' will presumably here be a second allusion to the

financial support received. But the qualification of this *koinōnia* as 'participation in the *Gospel*' shows at once that Paul is thinking of more than merely that, and this becomes all the plainer when he goes on 'from the first day until now'. Chrysostom recalls the work of the trainer and his assistants in the preparation of the athlete, through which they have part in his 'crown'. Their personal part with *him*, Paul means to say, is participation in the shame, but also in the glory, of his *message*. *Hence* there is cause to thank *God* for them. And in speaking of such 'participation in the Gospel' he will surely also have been thinking not only of gifts of money and such like, but of the active collaboration of the Philippians in the *proclaiming* of the Gospel, of their earnestness in letting it *be* Gospel in their own midst, of their *prayers* for its progress through the world and *to that extent* their company on his own high, hard apostolic way. But if this way according to v. 7 is *grace* and the *synkoinōnia* (copartnership) of which the Philippians have given active proof is thus 'copartnership in *grace*', then it is obvious that as the third and inmost of the concentric circles in which this *synkoinōnia* is to be understood, Zwingli's interpretation must also be explicitly adopted: *populus qui evangelio credit* (the people which *believe* the Gospel). That they have had access 'from the first day until now' to the *grace* in which he, the apostle, stands (Rom. 5.2), *that* is strictly and ultimately what he gives thanks for—certainly also for the help they had just given and certainly also for their Christian zeal in general, but for these things surely only because he can give thanks *for that*.

6 might well be the authentic commentary on the word 'joy' in v. 4, an unequivocal confirmation of the meaning we found above in the apostle's thanksgiving as a whole. Paul gives thanks, **putting my confidence in this, that he who has begun the good work among you will complete it.** So Paul does not marvel where there is only the transitory to marvel at. He gives thanks and he rejoices, because he *is confident*. His confidence, however, is not in the Christianity of the Philippians, which in itself deserves no more confidence than anything else that is human. But 'this confidence comes of God's persuading, from the instruction and

guardian admonition of the Word' (Horn). His confidence is—
the Philippians after all only provide cause and impulse to worship
God—in him who does not tire of giving, nor become incapable
of it, who does not abandon the work of his hands, as men without exception and for good reasons are wont somehow to do,
and that not only at their death. But he who alone possesses im-
mortality (I Tim. 6.16) is also he who alone keeps faith. In *him*
Paul's confidence is placed. It was not Paul who 'began the good
work' in Philippi, nor did the Philippians themselves do so by
becoming converted. God began it. That strips them and him of
all glory, *all* self-assurance, but precisely therewith also of all
despondency, all inquisitorial deliberation as to whether everyone
in Philippi is still as much in earnest as ever and will always remain so, whether they will keep faith and not perhaps forsake the
way upon which they have entered. It is a question of *God's*
earnestness, *God's* good faith, *God's* way—and there is certainly *no*
question about him, whatever the state of the Philippians may be.
Paul believes (for himself as for the others) in the sanctification
with which God hallows the *un*holy. That does not prevent his
rejoicing all the same in what these lost creatures are and do, seeing
the light of God among them, being thankful for it. On the contrary, it prevents his letting himself be robbed of that joy (*and* of
the courage also to speak sternly to them if need be) by making
human, all-too-human calculations of the possibilities given them.
He who has begun *this* 'good work', will also complete it.[1]

Complete it **until the day of Christ Jesus.** The work of God
that sanctifies our life's day takes place within bounds. The
boundary is the day of the Lord and his new, final work in us.
Reconciliation points beyond itself to redemption. But here and
now, within the bounds, the work of reconciliation wrought in
the same Lord must be completed in us through his Spirit. That is
the 'completing' of which Paul here speaks. Notice *what* it is that
is here set as our life's goal. We have here the point made forty
years ago by Friedrich Zündel (following in the steps of the elder
Blumhardt) and cast by him with at first such remarkably little

---

[1] That we have to recognize in the *ergon agathon* (the good work) of v. 6 a
further allusion to the pecuniary assistance (Dibelius), is really hardly plausible.

success into the theological debate on the New Testament. It is not the day of our death, our blessed departure from this world that forms the end, but the day of Christ Jesus, his victory in this world, its creation anew by him—the day of our death only in so far as it coincides for us with that day, and therefore so far as it means for us not *our escape*, but the *coming of the Lord* into the transitory world. And thus too the completion which Paul calls the aim of our life cannot consist in our being perfected for a safe departure from this vale of tears, but in our being fashioned to the hand of the God who triumphs over all tears and makes a new creation. Thus the 'work' that *he* has begun among us urges us perforce away from all resignation, including all Christian resignation, to *hope*.

7-8. **Right and proper,** Paul calls it, **to think this of you all.** It is an objective order[1] that binds Paul to the Philippians in the way described (thanksgiving, joy, intercession, confidence). This bond exists *rightly* and of *necessity*, **because I bear you in my heart,** because they are not far from him but as near as he is to himself. But how can he say that of them 'all', except as an empty phrase—of these many, distant people, for the most part certainly personally unknown to him, though in part perhaps only too well known? Does any such togetherness exist—not with definite individuals, nor with friends, not with loved ones in the human sense, but with an unlimited number, with mere fellowmen, with people who in the human sense may in many respects be the opposite of loved ones? A togetherness which then yields such a vision of the best in the other—not of his human but of his divine conditionality, potentiality and hope? Paul says he loves the Philippians **as those who in my imprisonment, as also in my defence and declaration of the Gospel, are my copartners in grace.** Copartners in grace: that is the secret of this love—and of this whole paragraph. At the time he writes this letter Paul is suffering in prison (we hold to the usual view that this was his last, *Roman* imprisonment). But *in* this imprisonment, namely in

---

[1] Again it seems to me out of place to see with Dibelius in the *dikaion* (right) a reference to the offering in question.

the court proceedings that are now going on (or in the interrup-
tions of his imprisonment?—the terms could also be meant
generally, in the sense of Acts 28.31), he is active in the public
presentation of the Gospel. This two-sided situation he calls *grace*.
In the fact that as an apostle he must suffer in this way and may act
in this way (cf. vv. 19 ff.), he sees the great wonder that is God's
merciful disposition towards men applied quite individually and
concretely to *himself*. This happens to him, and this he must do,
because God is gracious to him. Were God not gracious, then
there would be no such suffering and action in the world. And
from the fact that *he* must suffer and act in such a way, he gathers
that God is gracious to *him*. But just because it is grace, he knows
and sees he is not alone. Does it not bind him to all the 'holy',
even as it has made him the apostle to all the unholy whom God is
pleased also to call 'holy'? The Philippians have made it easy for
him not to know but to *see* this 'partnership' in grace. Through
their participation in all he suffers and does, they have made themselves known to him. As what? As loving and lovable people?
No: as the beloved *of God*, as fellow-recipients of grace. Were
they not *with* him in receiving grace, then they would not participate in all he suffers and does. And thus: it is because *God* obviously bears them in his heart, that *Paul* does so too, that it seems to
him also 'right and proper' ('just' is the literal word, and perhaps
after all the more pregnant one too in translation!) to think of
them all in the way described in vv. 6-7. Grace has made them his
copartners. Once more this is confirmed in what follows.

8 shows the necessity of this interpretation of v. 7. Paul calls **God**
to **witness how greatly I long for you all.** Love for someone
who is absent is longing, and that bitter, consuming longing for
his personal presence. Else it is not real love. Where men really
love each other they cannot get on without each other as easily as
not, but only in case of necessity. Paul does not hesitate to describe
his relation to the Philippians as real love of this kind. But his
calling on the name of God at once breaks through the limits of
what we otherwise know as real love. God can stand witness for
Paul's longing because it is his grace that forms directly the bond

of the union which is the true reason for that longing. Here we have men in real human love desiring not to be separated but to be together, but that is because as lost creatures they have found themselves together before God in his grace.

Paul longs for the Philippians **with the affection of Christ Jesus.** Bengel here observes: *in Paulo non Paulus vivit, sed Jesus Christus; quare Paulus non in Pauli sed Jesu Christi movetur visceribus* (in Paul it is not Paul that lives, but Jesus Christ; wherefore Paul is moved not by Paul's but by Jesus Christ's affection—literally *splagchna = viscera*, 'bowels, heart').[1] The slave (v. 1) recalls his *Lord*, in whose service he stands and whom in his human way he loves. It is obviously not the strength and intensity[2] of this 'affection' that is to be brought out by the addition 'of Christ Jesus', but its *uniqueness* and *peculiarity*. Its uniqueness: though it is not ashamed to appear in the form of a genuine human emotion, yet its motive power is the grace of God in Christ as that grace is proclaimed and believed in the community of the holy. Its peculiarity: if like all real love it seeks the presence of the beloved, yet it seeks him as the love of Jesus seeks men, without that self-seeking that seems to cling like a curse to even the most real human love, seeks him for God's sake and thus in the deepest sense for his own sake.

9–II. And my prayer is, Paul goes on, taking up again the thread of vv. 3–4. Precisely *because* he addresses them as 'copartners in grace', he is then *concretely* in earnest in his thinking of them (v. 3), in his hopeful view of the completion of the divine work begun among them (v. 6), in the affection with which he longs for them (v. 8). He knows what he would say to them and wish for them if he were with them and could speak to them. He must and will intercede for them, and his intercession, like all his prayer, can never be anything but a *total* concern. 'This life has not yet reached the end it is to attain . . . . but we have only a breakfast

---

[1] Apart from the nasty expression I agree with Dibelius, as against Ewald-Wohlenberg, that the passage is concerned with Paul's 'mystical communion' with Christ.

[2] Lueken's translation *Herzinnigkeit* (fondheartedness, heartfelt ardour) obviously turns the thing into sentimentalism.

and a foretaste of the same', says Luther here,[1] and once more
Bengel: *ignis in apostolo nunquam dicit: sufficit* (the inner fire in the
apostle never says: now it is enough). This end to the paragraph
might well make its beginning wholly unmistakable.—But to
continue: **my prayer is, that your love may increase more
and more.** That *their love* is to increase in knowledge, etc., as it is
presently put, seems difficult. Hence at the time of the Reformation some exegetes, e.g. Zwingli, succumbed to the temptation to
translate *hē agapē hymōn* by 'Your Graces'.[2] 'Love' will have to be
taken here as a concentrated expression for the highest, ultimate
human potentiality which Paul sees realized in the Philippians as
members of the body of Christ: they love. But they are on earth,
in the flesh, on the way. That is why their love has to be prayed
for, that it may increase. All ideas of a growing *quantity* will have
to be *avoided* here. *Perisseuein* means of course: to overflow, super-
abound, and thus in fact to go beyond measure, surpass all
measurement. Love must 'increase' in quality, in its orientation
towards the 'day of Christ' mentioned anew in v. 10. It is for that
very reason that the apostolic intercession is concerned with the
whole—not with a desirable partial improvement in their Christianity but with a drive forward, with *the* drive forward, with the
situation in *all* its seriousness.

Paul says: your love must increase—no: I *pray* for you that it
may increase **in knowledge and all-round discernment to
distinguish what really matters.** *Epignōsis* (basic clarity of
thinking) and *aisthēsis* (capacity for practical, concrete judgment)
both point to its being a case of love's 'increasing' in certainty
with respect to its *Object*. That their love should understand itself
ever better, that the eternal, holy, merciful God who at the end
of our days will perform his new work upon us should be understood more and more as the Beloved—that is the 'increase' Paul
begs for them. And this 'increase' would have to manifest itself in
the exercise of a faculty to *distinguish* what matters and what does

---

[1] *Works*, Erl. edn, 9.333.
[2] '*Euer Liebden*' has no direct equivalent in English. It was a form of address
used between sovereigns, constructed on the same principle as 'Your Grace',
'Your Worship', etc. but from the root 'love' (*Translator*).

not matter when this God is the Object of our love. 'That small things should as small be seen, and great things great to us should seem', that we do not fall for truths, precepts and catchwords that are none, that we take steady steps—towards that goal.

Paul does not become more concrete than that for the moment. He will later. But we sense his concrete concern here already from the conclusion: **so that you may be pure and faultless against the day of Christ, filled with fruits of the righteousness which is** (created) **through Jesus Christ, to the glory and praise of God.** What it means to be 'pure and faultless against the day of Christ', at the dawning of the day that is the goal of our days, would seem at first to be an open *question*. But the question answers itself when we recall from v. 6 *who* it is who begins and completes the 'work' directed towards that day. On no account can it then mean an integrity and intactness which we have to bring about ourselves. That would rather fall under the impurity and fault of which a knowing and discerning love will *not* make itself guilty. Pure and faultless is rather the man who in his lack of integrity renders faith and obedience to that work of God. This finding is confirmed by the sequel, or explanation, 'filled with fruits of the righteousness which is through Jesus Christ'. The truth about this righteousness is unequivocally taught by vv. 3, 6, 9. It is God's righteousness, righteousness that is *believed in*, or in fact, as it is here put no less precisely, righteousness *through Christ*. Hence not through us! If that is so, then its 'fruits' also, of which it is here said that on the ground of that knowing and discerning love we are to be 'filled' with them, cannot be different in kind. 'Fruit' of *this* righteousness can only consist in our *abiding* by God's righteousness all along the line, acquiescing in the fact that *he* is righteous. It is 'to the glory and praise of God'[1] that we are finally to stand pure and faultless at the appearance of the day of Christ. That does not exclude, but includes: to our own *shame*—yet in our disgrace believing in *him*, obeying *him*. Everything depends on *this* purity, *this* faultlessness. Everything depends on their remaining 'copartners in *grace*',

[1] A conclusion in which we certainly may not see with Dibelius merely 'an overflowing rhetorical formula'.

not ceasing to cling to grace, to follow the pull of grace. Therein lies their purity and faultlessness, and only therein. The urgent *admonition* which here turns out to be the content of the apostolic intercession seems to contrast strangely with vv. 3-5. But the beginning and the end of our paragraph are sprung from the same root. The former is not to be understood without the latter, nor the latter without the former, and both only from the cardinal passage in v. 6, in which thanksgiving and supplication, joy and care, peace and passion flow together and ever and again spring in two.

For you must know, brethren, that what has happened to me has amounted rather to an advance of the Gospel: my imprisonment has certainly become publicized in Christ in the praetorium and among all the rest, and certainly most of the brethren—deriving from my imprisonment confidence in the Lord—have found greater courage to speak the Word of God without fear. Some, it is true, proclaim Christ also from envy and jealousy, others also out of goodwill—from love, realizing that I am appointed for the defence of the Gospel, the latter preach Christ; the former out of contentiousness, insincerely, with the idea of afflicting me prisoner as I am. What does it matter? Except that one way or the other, whether deceitfully or sincerely, Christ is preached! And in that I rejoice. And I shall rejoice! For I know: 'This will turn out to my salvation'. Through your prayers and through the support of the Spirit of Jesus Christ, according to my expectation and my hope: I shall by no means be put to shame, but in all openness, as always so also now, Christ will be magnified through my bodily life, be it in life or be it in death. For to me to live is Christ and to die is gain. But if it is to be life in the flesh, then that means to me a harvest. I know not which I should choose. I have both on my mind: I desire to depart and be with Christ—how much better that would be!—but to remain in the flesh is more necessary for your sakes. And since that is what I count on, I think I shall remain, remain with you all to your increase and joy in the faith, that your courage in Christ Jesus may increase through me —through my coming to you again.

3-11 have shown us Paul's first reaction to the anxious participation of the Philippians in his personal lot. Thanksgiving to *God* and prayer for God's work in *them* is his instinctive answer—superior, but in its very superiority tranquillizing. Yet Paul is no

Stoic, as in this very letter we shall often enough have occasion to observe; he certainly does not mean by this answer to pass non-chalantly over the actual blackness of his situation and the anxiety that fills the Philippians on his account.[1] Even the surprising description of his situation as 'grace' in v. 7 is not to be left standing as a paradoxical assertion, but is to be made meaningful for the readers by being explained in concrete terms. So now he will give them a direct answer to their direct question about what has happened to him, about the present and probable future state of his affairs. This second answer we have before us in vv. 12-26.

12. The opening, **For you must know, brethren,** calls our attention, as happens wherever Paul uses this or a similar phrase, to the fact that what he is now about to say is also something which the readers, at least at first sight, will *not* find self-evident—so that to that extent we have here a counterpart to the 'I however *thank* our Lord' of vv. 3-11. With *ta kat' eme,* **what has happened to me,** Paul sums up everything the readers had apparently asked about in the first instance. He will now in fact tell them what he has experienced in Rome, and what has happened to him there—that is to say, to him as an apostle of Christ. To that extent his second answer is a direct answer. He will not speak of the human whys and wherefores. Epaphroditus the bearer of the letter (2.25 ff.) and later on Timothy (2.19 ff.) can tell them about that by word of mouth. To that extent his second answer, too, is an indirect answer. He answers above all in such a way as to put the readers' question tacitly into the right form, the only appropriate one: they had of course asked about what had happened to him, the apostle as such. To this question the brethren *must* indeed have an answer from Paul himself. For 'through the coming of Jesus Christ into the world we poor sinners are entwined in the sufferings and victories of the eternal Word' (Horn). What Paul experiences as an apostle concerns the Philippians as directly as does the Gospel itself, because it is in fact nothing else but the *course* of the Gospel. So we now understand what follows:

[1] 'This, too, is evidence of love: that, anxious as they were about him, he gives them information about his situation' (Chrysostom).

Rather, *mallon* writes Paul as a distinct correction of the presupposed question—they **have amounted rather to an advance
of the Gospel,** the things that have happened *to me.* Though the
readers might perhaps complain that their anxiety lest his affairs
might be humanly speaking in a bad, or even very bad way was
not removed by this answer, nor even by the hopeful expressions
of 1.25 f.; 2.24, yet his apostolic objectivity prevents Paul's discussing the matter further. He just would not be an apostle if he
could speak objectively about his own situation in abstraction
from the course of the Gospel, to which he has sacrificed his subjectivity and therewith also all objective interest in his person. To
the question how it is with *him* an apostle *must* react with information as to how it is with the *Gospel.* And so Paul now answers by
declaring that with the Gospel it is at all events *well.* What has
happened to him, the apostle, has amounted to an advance, a drive
forward, a territorial gain for his message and cause. That amounts
to saying that with him, the apostle, whatever his human prospects may be, it is *well.* The human aspect is not suppressed: it is
there, but the eye that sees it is the eye of the 'slave of Christ
Jesus' (1.1) who sees the human element moved and ordered
according to the will and plan of his Lord. He sees it in the service
of the eternal Word, and it is *to that extent* that it interests him.
There will also be provision made for the imprisoned Jew in
Rome with *his* sufferings and joys to get a hearing. But first of all
we must follow the apostle on *his* track. Thus: things are not
going badly with the Gospel but well, not backwards but forwards. It has not suffered a blow through what has happened to
me, but it has triumphed anew. That is what he tells us first of all.
But how far is that so? The answer is given by vv. 13-14:

**My imprisonment has certainly become publicized in
Christ in the praetorium and among all the rest.** In view of
the scantiness of our knowledge of all the concrete details, which
can hardly be remedied by Acts 28, it will be well to abide by
this simple translation and interpretation of the passage.[1] Paul's

[1] Older exegetes, foremost among them Hofmann, and more recent ones
like Schlatter and Ewald-Wohlenberg, have ventured to derive the following
meaning from these verses: Paul is here saying: in consequence of the court

imprisonment has become in Rome a well-known and much talked-of affair. It has acted contrary to its intention as a lampstand for the Light. Everything depends on that—that is why Paul says explicitly: my imprisonment was publicized *in Christ*. By praetorium we are to understand not a building but the *occupants* of a building, and in fact, if we are agreed that the scene is not set in Caesarea or Ephesus, the occupants of the barracks of the imperial life guard, where state prisoners of Paul's kind seem to have been interned. 'All the rest' will then be a somewhat vague expression for 'the widest circles'. We could perhaps render freely, 'among the praetorians and throughout the whole of society my imprisonment is the topic of the day'. Paul would naturally not call such 'becoming publicized' in itself an 'advance of the Gospel'. It is here that the 'in Christ' comes in decisively. Through the power *of Christ* who indeed is the immediate cause of this imprisonment and the Lord of this prisoner, and as a piece of witness *for him* who intends to glorify himself through this imprisonment and in this prisoner, Paul's case has not remained in the sphere of an obscure lawsuit that concerns only those immediately involved. On the contrary, the *fact* of his imprisonment has become a *Word* that is at all events *noised abroad*, a *problem* which troubles the neighbourhood

proceedings now begun, which had brought him into the praetorium, the quarters of the imperial guard—a circumstance which the Philippians had allowed to cause them unnecessary alarm—it had rather come to light and to everyone's ears that he was a prisoner 'in Christ' (v. 13) and not because of a common crime dangerous to the state. This was a great gain for the cause of the Gospel and had had the result that the Roman Christians had 'found courage in the Lord' to take up the Christian proclamation anew and without fear, since now, in view of Paul, there was no danger of their possibly being prosecuted for it under the criminal law. It will be better *not* to join in this interpretation, however lucid the passage may thereby become. Whether the court, and therewith also the Roman public, appreciated the fact that Paul's activity took place 'in Christ' and could therefore well be temporarily suspicious, but not politically dangerous, is a question which could surely be decided at best by the *outcome* of the trial (which seems, however, to have been entirely different), not right at its opening. That the Roman Christians would then have 'taken courage in the Lord' to preach fearlessly—because there was now no more risk in so doing, is a second very remarkable presupposition of this interpretation. And finally, the formula 'in Christ', on which all the emphasis would then fall, has a meaning thereby read into it which is certainly not impossible in itself, but in view of its position in the sentence (after *phanerous*, public) is not really probable.

—and that not only the immediate neighbourhood—and stirs them up to think and question. And Paul will surely have had even more in mind than that: this Word has been heard, it has proved itself not only a problem but a real power, it has met with not only interest but *faith*. It surely could not be otherwise, when the matter became publicized 'in Christ': the circle of those who are judged and accepted 'in Christ' has through God's mercy become larger.

That brings us to the second thing Paul thinks of when he speaks of the 'advance of the Gospel': **certainly most of the brethren—deriving from my imprisonment confidence in the Lord—have found greater courage to speak the Word of God without fear.** The majority of the Roman congregation, which of course was not founded by Paul and thus had no direct connection with the illustrious prisoner, have grasped the situation, or rather: the situation has been 'publicized in Christ' to them also, has become for them too a Word from the Lord. The arrest of Paul has not had a deterrent or intimidating effect on them, but the *phanerōsis* (the publicity), the Word of Christ that came alive in Rome through his presence as prisoner and defendant giving a public account of himself—that has found new ears and tongues also among them. Once more they venture further forward than they have evidently done for a time.[1] The Word spoken in their midst through the imprisonment of the apostle has awakened in them, too, the old insight that 'Christianity' is no private hole-and-corner business but a matter of thoroughly and specifically public concern, and must also be represented by 'Christians' as such. The light, the movement, the power that proceeded from the prisoner's testimony has automatically put the Word of God once more on their lips as well, and made them employ their freedom more fearlessly than ever amid the indifference of the metropolis and its hostility to the truth. That is the other thing in which Paul sees the *prokopē*, the advance of the Gospel in Rome.

[1] 'From the *perissoterōs* "greater" (courage) it follows that earlier on, too, they were of good courage and preached undismayed, but now far more so' (Chrysostom).

15-18a have been rightly described[1] as an *excursus*. This second point in which Paul sees the triumph of his imprisonment, i.e. of the Christ who manifests himself in him, was not without its dark side. It was certainly not as if the Roman congregation, as they saw among them the man who was now the source of the said movement in pagan society and in their own midst; the man who had once written them from Corinth the Epistle to the Romans, had somehow come to regard him with unanimous thoughts of brotherliness, sympathy and even veneration. The general esteem for Paul as *the* apostle of Jesus Christ set in relatively late in Christendom—at a time when *no* characteristic picture of his nature and ways any longer existed. During his lifetime it was *not* accorded him. The name Paul in the days when its bearer could still be met face to face and was less easily translated into harmless terms than later, stood for something that was opposed by many. The grounds for that were manifold. There were 'Christian' persuasions which were so publicly and vigorously combatted by Paul that their supporters can hardly be blamed if they saw in him more their *opponent* than their Christian 'brother'. This attitude was of course entirely mutual. We might further suppose that in the Christian congregations there were everywhere some who, without any intentional attack on Paul's part, *felt* themselves attacked or cold-shouldered through 'his' Gospel (Rom. 2.16; 16.25). From documents like the second half of II Corinthians we can further see that it was definitely just not easy to reconcile oneself to the man's *personal* manner.[2] However that may be: in Rome, according to vv. 15-18, he was made to feel the consequences of his singular and much-disputed position —a doubly painful experience at the moment when he was aware that by giving public account of himself in Rome of all places he was entering on the decisive phase of his apostolate. That is the melancholy fact which he reports to Philippi as an appendix to the news of the 'advance' of the Gospel: the preaching of Christ in

[1] By Dibelius.
[2] 'He was known as a man who had brought trouble and difficulties wherever he went, so that there was probably not a single place where he left behind unanimously good memories' (Horn).

Rome, which according to vv. 13-14 had received new stimulus through his presence, was at least in part decidedly anti-Pauline preaching. The picture of this fact cannot well be made clearer for us than Paul, speaking here as he does with a certain reserve, happens to have drawn it. Twice—the second time evidently in order to be somewhat more concrete than the first, and this time in the reverse order—he paints in vv. 15-17 the two-sided situation: the Roman Christians who were unfriendly in what they felt and said and those who were friendly.

Let us take up first the picture of the former. **Some proclaim Christ also from envy and jealousy,** it is said in v. 15—**out of contentiousness** (*eritheia*), **insincerely** (i.e. not only with pertinent intent), **with the idea of thereby afflicting me prisoner as I am** (literally, of thereby adding affliction on top of my imprisonment), so v. 17 begins (in the version underlying Luther's translation [and the AV and RV] v. 16)—and they are again reproached in v. 18 with preaching Christ **deceitfully** (*prophasei*). We know far too little about personalities and circumstances to expand these few strokes into a clearer picture. Only some misunderstandings can be corrected by means of these few strokes. For one thing this: the picture of the situation is not drawn in the simple black and white in which it has often been reproduced. The double *kai* (also) in v. 15 must be noticed. It could of course also mean merely an intensification of the words *dia phthonon kai erin* (from envy and jealousy) and *di' eudokian* (in goodwill). Yet I find it more probable that Paul wishes to indicate that it is *not only* from envy and jealousy that they proclaim Christ, as indeed also the *eudokia* (goodwill) of the others towards Paul is not their sole motive. Paul says there are tendencies present in the Roman preaching of the Gospel that are disagreeable, directed against himself.[1] But yet he evidently sees even in his opponents not only that. We shall have to bear in mind this *kai* (also) when we come to the more exclusive-sounding passage in 2.21: 'They all seek their own, not that which is of Christ Jesus!', which seems also to refer, at least partially, to

[1] 'In the behaviour of some men who had a certain standing in the Roman congregation jealousy came to light' (Schlatter).

this wider circle of the people about the apostle in Rome.

A further point is: the opposition in which they set themselves to Paul, and in which he himself regards them, is *not of a material kind*. Some have thought it necessary to recognize in the opponents in question anti-Paulinists in the sense of Galatians and in the sense of Phil. 3.2 f.—Judaizers, probably no other than the fanatical vegetarians with whom he had dealt in Rom. 14-15. That is out of the question:[1] how Paul managed opponents who came from that quarter preaching 'another' Gospel, is known to us from Gal. 1; II Cor. 11; Col. 2; and not least Phil. 3 where Paul shows really and truly that the old warrior has not grown any milder in that respect, and that for all the 'moderation' (*epieikes*, 4.5) he recommends and exercises in this letter, he is on the watch with his usual vigour where *that* opposition is concerned. To people of *that* kind he would not three times (vv. 15, 17, 18) have conceded in due form that they proclaim *Christ*. The 'in that I rejoice' of v. 18 would then be in Paul's mouth a sheer impossibility. It must have been a case of *personal* unfriendliness or of such material opposition as Paul, at least from his side, could enter into discussion over, of *articuli* NON *fundamentales* (of *non*-fundamental points of doctrine) as it was put in the seventeenth century. The expressions *phthonos* (envy) and *eris* (jealousy) in v. 15, and *eritheia* (contentiousness) in v. 17, make for the conjecture that it was to a great extent questions of prestige that brought part of the Roman Christians into opposition to him. The 'afflicting of the man who is in prison' in v. 17 will also be most simply explained to this effect: 'They fight for their honour and their views, form a special group and set to work in order to be able to assert themselves alongside of Paul and over against him. And to this end they think they can now perhaps utilize also his hampered condition as a prisoner' (Schlatter).

Be that as it may—however much the matter obviously pained him, it was certainly not such as to give him cause to become *intransigent*, or 'tragic'. That is surely ruled out by the fact that the

---

[1] It is naturally even more wide of the mark to suspect them outright of being secret agents of some kind, 'non-believers' who by their preaching of Christ sought to goad the emperor to violent persecution (Chrysostom).

picture of Roman Christianity is a two-sided one: fortunately, and to his joy, there is no lack of such as **proclaim Christ also out of goodwill** (namely, towards him) v. 15—**from love** (to him), **since they know that I am appointed** (ordained by God, as the *keimai* is to be understood) **for the defence of the Gospel,** v. 16—they proclaim Christ **in truth** (here doubtless = without mental reservations and ulterior motives) v. 18. That is the other, the fair and encouraging side of the situation. Not everyone takes the significance of the moment to be that now the great thing is to get clear of Paul, to refuse to be put in the shade by him, to rival his achievements: in Rome, too, his special mission is not only misjudged, the decisive significance of his rendering public account of himself precisely here is also *understood*, he has men around him and behind him in this congregation which others founded, and knows himself upheld and supported by them. A *third* reason for us not to paint ourselves *too* gloomy a picture of the situation.

18a is doubtless one of the finest samples of what can be called the Pauline *superiority*: that wholly objective concentration of interest which, despite all the passion apparent here as elsewhere for the dignity of his special mission, has yet become his deepest nature— so that he can still freely survey from an ultimate standpoint the personal questions of for and against by which he is surrounded. **What does it matter** (the attitude of the Roman preachers for or against him)? What can it matter, **except that one way or the other** (whatever their intentions) **Christ is preached.** Not that the situation did not distress him—one cannot fail to recognize that it did—but beyond the pleasantness or unpleasantness with which it affects him personally, he sees the result: Christ *is* preached in Rome. The preaching of Christ is the axis and the whole question of for and against Paul is one of the questions that revolve round it. He holds to that axis. If he has only more or less confidence in men and their motives, he has *complete* confidence in him who is their Lord as well as his, and also in the work executed with strange tools by his hand. **In that I rejoice.** For that is in fact the 'advance' of the Gospel (v. 12) which has resulted from his situation. For himself it is in more than one respect not at all an enjoyable event: but he has no wish to be consulted about what *for him* is enjoyable. So he rejoices in the 'advance' itself, in the spread of the Word, however those who speak it may be disposed towards him personally.

Once again: there can be no question at this point of any indifference towards opposition of a material kind to his message. Where that is the issue we shall hear just as sharp tones in Philippians as anywhere else. But perhaps one may venture the biographical remark that we have here to do with an insight that has grown and matured in comparison with, say, II Corinthians— with the insight that it was possible in a dispute to take the object of the dispute *more* seriously than he had done before, the accompanying personal aspects *still less* seriously, and so to adopt *in* the dispute a standpoint *above* the dispute, or if not to adopt it then at least to see it and assert its validity. The 'joy' to which Paul here confesses can be legitimate joy because he is rejoicing *neither* in his opponents *nor* in himself but in the power of the object to which he subordinates himself and them—because he rejoices in the fact that, as he later says, also in this context, 'Christ will be magnified.'

18b-20. Now, having said what was necessary about the *prokopē* (advance) of the Gospel and the things connected with it, he returns to his situation in general. **And I shall rejoice!** he begins in v. 18b, connecting naturally with the preceding *kai en toutō chairō* (and in that I rejoice). The object in which Paul rejoices remains the same, but the ground of his rejoicing now shifts. The quotation from Job 13.16—**'This will turn out to my salvation'**—does not refer to the proclamation of the Gospel in Rome as it takes place before his eyes and in ways not unconnected with his presence there. It refers rather to the fact of his presence itself, which apparently (and that is what the Philippians are afraid of) could also turn out to something very different from his salvation. He is there as prisoner at the bar. What will become of him? Paul gives the answer in advance: 'I shall rejoice!' The connexion with the preceding 'I rejoice' is neither fortuitous nor arbitrary, despite the extension of the ground for Paul's rejoicing.

Here, too, the *object* of rejoicing is that great axis round which all personal questions and all earthly human fates ultimately revolve. He saw it in what for him personally is the somewhat questionable preaching of the Roman theologians; he sees it now also in the uncertain possibilities of his own future. With the same superiority with which he held to the fact that 'Christ is proclaimed', he says here: this—that is, everything that my present position as prisoner at the bar can bring me—will it turn out to my salvation? *Oida*, I *know* it will.

Two things will help towards its being so: **your prayers and the support of the Spirit of Jesus Christ.** Notice the juxtaposition of these two factors. The *Spirit*, who will not forsake him, who will be present in word and action come what may, because he cannot be untrue to himself whatever may happen to the man Paul, is the Lord in Person, the divine Self who cannot tolerate that these happenings should somehow *not* turn out to his salvation. But the prayers of the Philippians are not too paltry, not too human, not too powerless to stand beside this first factor, although beside it, strictly speaking, no second can stand. On the contrary, in its neighbourhood they become an absolute factor in themselves. It is just the same with the two concepts by which Paul in v. 20 describes the ground on which the knowledge of v. 19 is based. I know it, **according to my expectation and my hope.** *Apokaradokia* ('looking out for something with head held high') describes in Rom. 8.19, the only New Testament parallel, the great waiting of the creation, of all things finite, for the redemption from transience which breaks in with the 'manifestation of the sons of God'. In the neighbourhood of the concept *hope*, in which of course for Paul the object hoped for is itself already included, this 'expectation' is likewise not some sort of empty anticipation that may be mocked, but like the prayer of the congregation a waiting fraught with actualization, a questioning fraught with answer, a hoping fraught with fulfilment.

That is why Paul **knows.** He knows: **I shall by no means be put to shame.** That is not to say anything at all about his fate: it can turn one way or another, but over every possible fate there stands the future—present—triumph of the coming redemption.

The 'being put to shame' must also be taken here in a strictly objective sense. Paul really believes he does not know how his case will end. That he expresses an optimistic view of it in 2.24 does not alter the fact that at bottom, as is later plain, he takes both possibilities into consideration. 'To be put to shame' does not mean, to lose the case and therewith his life, but to fall from the grace of v. 7, which consists in his being permitted to speak of God and witness for God. He lives in that, and knows it, *indestructibly*. None will take it from him, as none either can give him it. *For that reason*, as a recipient of grace, he lives in an expectation and hope that are really already fulfilled; *for that reason* he is certain both of the power of the Philippians' intercession and of the Spirit's support.

But the opposite is also true: because grace is *grace*, he must expect and hope. For the same reason the Philippians should pray and the Spirit must support him, that he be not put to shame, that every eventuality he may have to face should become a confirmation of his calling: that **in all openness**[1] (so it must be taken, as in Col. 2.15; John 7.4; 11.54, not as 'boldness', which does not give good sense in this context), *whatever may happen* (it can only be a case of the confirmation of grace, the actualization of the awaited object!), **Christ should be magnified through my bodily life** (as Schlatter translates it), **whether through life or death.** Notice the passive, *megalynthēsetai* (will be made great). Paul sees himself entirely as object: it was not to an action but to a happening that his argument has been leading up. His somatic (psychocorporal) earthly life is a means which, so he hopes and prays, Christ will at all events use for the extension of *his* power and glory. He has used it thus far 'in all openness': 'I do not dare,' he writes in Rom. 15.18-19, 'to say anything (about my doings) that was not performed through me by *Christ*, to bring the heathen to obedience, by word and deed in the power of signs and wonders, in the power of the Holy Spirit—so that in a circle from Jerusalem as far as Illyria I have completed the proclamation of the Gospel'. That was *till now* the magnifying of Christ in all openness through the bodily life of Paul. Now the court case lies ahead of him. It is

[1] In the sense of 'publicity', not of 'frankness' (*Translator*).

not to be taken for granted—and must therefore be hoped and prayed for—that this will continue to happen 'now also'. Let him be acquitted and summoned anew to active life—or else let him be condemned and fall a prey to the power of death! Christ can be magnified through both and in both. Both can mean a new *prokopē tou euangeliou* (a new advance of the Gospel). Notice too how the decisive expression 'magnifying of Christ through my bodily life' in itself could very well be a description of the resurrection of the dead (3.21). In that light at all events, to be in life or in death a confessor before men is to have the splendour and significance of a goal to which Paul looks forward in hope. Its splendour is the splendour reflected from beyond the boundary of human life.[1] It is for that reason, and ultimately only for that reason, that Paul considers he can write to Philippi regarding his dark future: I rejoice and *shall* rejoice.

21-23. 'Christ will be magnified through my bodily life, whether it be in life or in death.' Does that really give any information about the present and future condition of the man Paul? Whatever is to be said on *that* subject is at any rate here set in the framework of information of a very different kind. Where life and death can thus be stood side by side as equals while *above* them, transcending and encompassing them, this third factor can appear of such sole importance, there indeed it is the *resurrection* that is being proclaimed, the glory of the Lord at the goal of all human existence and non-existence, beside which the outcome of Paul's trial, which is supposed to be the real topic of conversation, appears the merest shadow. This suppression of the minor theme by the greater one, the only one that matters, is the point of the tremendous build-up of ideas in vv. 19-20. It is only against that *background* that Paul would have the Philippians see his personal fate—just as he will also set what he has to say to them about themselves, as we shall see at once in the next section, against the most comprehensive of backgrounds so that it may be rightly seen.

But for the moment he turns back to the foreground. Vv. 21-23

---

[1] Cf. pp. 17 f. above (*Translator*).

form the transition, a kind of descent. As if he felt the harshness of
his last remark, he gives first of all an explanation of the alarming
'be it in death' of v. 20. How can it occur to me to say that the
goal of my highest and surest hope is, 'that Christ should be
magnified through my bodily life, be it in life or in death'? Even
in death? Does death mean just as much as life? Are they inter-
changeable ideas? Answer: **To me life** (what I really call my life!)
is Christ. The decisive commentary on this famous saying is
Gal. 2.20: 'I live, yet *no* longer *I* (*ouketi egō*), *Christ lives* in me'.
Thus the concept 'life' in v. 21 cannot be given the sense it undoubtedly bears in v. 20: life in the body, life of the man Paul in
himself, *this side* of the 'no longer I' of Gal. 2.20. To that, to his
'life in the flesh' as he will then explicitly call it, he will return in
v. 22. The *ei de* (but if) with which that sentence begins shows,
however, that he was speaking before of something else. *The* life
of Paul of which vv. 20 and 22 speak, has according to v. 21 been
checkmated so to speak (although it is still there on the board) by
another life. This other life is Christ himself. 'Even in my present
life it is not this that is my proper life, but Christ', as Chrysostom
paraphrases it. I live, but my life has been arrested and confiscated
by Christ and thus he lives for me, in my place, my proper life.
It is the same indirect identification—not of Paul with his Lord,
but of the Lord with his Paul—that is described in II Cor. 4.10 as
the life of Jesus in our body (*zōē tou Iēsou en tō sōmati hēmōn*), or in
II Cor. 4.16 as the inward man (*esō anthrōpos*), or in II Cor. 5.17 as
the new creation in Christ (*kainē ktisis en Christō*), or in Col. 3.3
as the hidden life with Christ in God (*syn tō Christō en tō theō*), or
likewise in Gal. 2.20 as the life by faith in the Son of God who
loved me and gave himself for me; or in II Cor. 5.15 as the life
which those for whom Christ died now live no longer unto
themselves—*mēketi heautois*—but to him who died and rose again
for them. Christ lives vicariously for me, as it could be summed
up. The expression 'Christ mysticism' would best be entirely
avoided.

Since, then, *this* life is to me *the* life, says Paul, therefore to me
to die is gain. To *this* life dying can only bring me gain, as it
will have to be explained Why gain? In v. 23 'to die' is described

as 'to depart and be with Christ'. Is it so self-evident as is usually supposed that these words, to take them up already here, really mean the same as the *endēmēsai pros ton kyrion*, the 'being at home with the Lord' of II Cor. 5.8? That it is a case of related ideas is of course indisputable. But it seems to me noteworthy that here, at any rate if the passage is to be expounded in its context, it is not as in II Cor. 5 a case of the contrast between the temporal, transient life and the eternal, intransient life for which Paul, hoping to have his tent broken up, to be clothed with the heavenly house and to be at home with the Lord, longs in a general sort of way, at least according to the beginning of that chapter (cf. however here, too, the above-quoted verses II Cor. 5.15, 17). Here it is rather a more concrete and special case of the significance of dying as gain, as increase, as expansion of Paul's life which is *Christ himself*, or which is identical with the 'magnifying' of Christ in v. 20. *Kerdos* (gain) in v. 21 surely cannot well be taken to mean that Paul hopes to be united with Christ in a life after death—as if he had not just described this union (*emoi to zēn Christos*, to me to live is Christ) as something already present—but it is to be related to the magnifying of Christ (*megalynthēsetai Christos*, v. 20). To gain Christ and be found in him (*Christon kerdainein kai heurethēnai en autō*) in 3.9 likewise surely does not mean to be together with Christ in eternal bliss (although that is *also* included) but first of all concretely, *Christi favorem et consortium consequi* (Grimm),[1] to attain the 'gain' of a life in completed fellowship with him. The *analysai*, the departure and leave-taking in order to die, means 'gain' because it means a perfect *syn Christō einai*, a 'being with Christ' now also in the death of the body, in dying with him—because Christ's 'being magnified' in the bodily life of his people is crowned by his taking them up also into *this 'einai syn autō'*, into the fellowship of his *death* (cf. 3.10). The 'gain' which Paul's life as a Christian receives by dying is the complement to the *hysterēmata tōn thlipseōn tou Christou*, 'what is still lacking in the afflictions of Christ', which Paul according to Col. 1.24 likewise rejoices to fill up by *his* sufferings.

It should be possible to see that the usual interpretation of v. 21,

[1] *Lexicon Graeco-Latinum in libros Novi Testamenti.*

which is also the interpretation presupposed in Simon Dach's well-known hymn ('longing for our eternal home', etc.), would take it completely out of the narrower and wider *context* of our epistle and also out of the joyful, courageous key of looking to Christ himself and not to a better life with him in the Beyond, would introduce a note that is certainly welcome at the usual kind of funeral service but is essentially foreign here; whereas with the interpretation just given we see the connexions with what goes before and after (not only with v. 20 but also e.g. with the view of suffering as *charis* in v. 7 and v. 29), and above all we then have the same manly, triumphant Paul before us here, too, as in the rest of the epistle. Did he not in v. 6 describe to the Philippians the 'day of Christ' as *terminus ad quem*, as the goal and end of their course? And should his own goal now be merely the heaven to which death is the gateway? No, let us rather say with the presumably authentic declaration of vv. 29-30: the grace which Paul here sees before him, and the prospect of which he there held out to the Philippians, consists in not only believing in Christ but also suffering for him. It could also be a secondary advantage of this interpretation of the passage, that then there is no further cause to make a to-do about the change that has allegedly come over the apostle's *eschatology* as compared with e.g. I Cor. 15, and to begin deliberations as to what sort of 'intermediate state' before the 'general' resurrection of the dead he could possibly have had in view in speaking of the *einai syn Christo* (the 'being with Christ') immediately after death. He is not in fact speaking at all about the life after death, but about the life of *Christ* and about what the death that perhaps awaits him might mean for that life.

Having now resolved the principal problem, we can be somewhat briefer in discussing the rest. In v. 22 Paul sets over against his death, over against the fellowship with Christ that is to be perfected by his 'departure', the **life in the flesh,** the continuance of corporal life—not of course to be confused with what in Rom. 8.4 f. is abhorred as 'walking after the flesh' or 'being in the flesh' or 'living to the flesh'. It means of course continuing to live *kata pneuma* (after the Spirit), as apostle, as servant of Christ, in that indirect identification with him of which we spoke, but—continuing to live, in the fellowship of Christ *without* its completion, checkmated but not yet taken off the board, in the garment of the *sarx*, of the flesh, which according to I Cor. 15 and II Cor. 5 undoubtedly means even for the Christian, even for the apostle, an ultimate restraint, a 'not yet', a deep concealment of the triumph of the Spirit dwelling within him. Paul means all that here. But he sees the possibility, the promise that even *this* life holds: but if it is to be life in the flesh, **then that means to me a harvest.** 'Life in the flesh' means 'reaping'. That is the possibility that would fall away in the event of his dying. That is why he can accept also the 'life in the flesh', if it is to be so. Why does he say 'reaping' and not 'labouring'? It most certainly does not look as if he thought merely to bring in fruits that were already grown, and no longer to plough and sow! The reason is, that again he is not really speaking at all of what *he* will suffer or do, but still on the same lines as v. 20 of the magnifying of Christ, in this case through continuing to live. Christ *has* ploughed and sown; his, the apostle's, earthly doings are the bringing in of the harvest of his labour. Thus the motive that makes continuing to live a thing of promise to him is not the officiously zealous sense of duty that is determined to keep going to the last breath of man and horse, but the gratitude that rejoices to reap where it has not sown. Christ the Lord is the possibility held also by his 'life in the flesh'.

Paul admits: **I know not which I should choose,** which of these two possibilities he should personally wish for himself.[1] He knows only that living or dying he is the Lord's (Rom. 14.8), waking or sleeping he lives with him (I Thess. 5.10). **I have both on my mind**[2] (Luther: 'I find both hard') v. 23. He is held in

---

[1] The *kai* at the beginning of v. 22b serves (as often with Paul) as an intensification of the word that follows, i.e. here of the *ti* or perhaps *hairēsomai*.

[2] Literally, 'Both are an *Anliegen* to me'. The word means 'an object of concern' and thus a trouble, anxiety or care, but also a wish or desire (hence the easy transition to 'desiring to depart') and sometimes even a burden (hence, presently, the idea of putting 'pressure' on him). Luther's expression, *beides liegt mir hart an*, is an old use of the same word in its verbal form, meaning 'both come hard to me'. The simplest English translation of the Greek is surely, 'I am torn between the two' (*Translator*).

check, so that he cannot grasp either the one or the other. Once more he envisages the first possibility: **I desire** to depart and be with Christ. So he does not merely sit on the fence between acceptance of the one and of the other, although he sees both possibilities held in one and the same hand, but he knows (and this is the pressure on him from the one side) that to die with Christ is *much* the greater—**how much better that would be!** —because it is the final, consummate act in which Christ can be glorified in his bodily life. But he has also had to assent to a further lease of life because it means further reaping in the service of the same Lord. That is what puts pressure on him from that side.

But (**24-26**)—the *decisive* thing when it comes to what he *will* do and what he 'confidently counts on' (*touto pepoithōs*, v. 25) is neither the greater nor the lesser 'desire' that he personally feels. He does not really need to choose at all, neither according to his better judgment as expressed in v. 23 nor against it. He sees what is **more necessary,** v. 24. We recall how he speaks in I Cor. 9.16 of the *anagkē* ('I *must* do it', Luther), the constraint laid on him to proclaim the Gospel. While he is deliberating, and finding no end to his deliberations, as to whether Christ is magnified more by his life or his death, he is of course—his congregations' apostle. He is that *now*; he is *not yet* in a position to glorify the Lord by his death. But it is certainly open to him **to remain in the flesh . . . for your sakes.** That is neither the 'gain' that causes his 'desire' to die nor the 'harvest' that causes his 'desire' to live. It is simply the *anagkē*, the necessity or constraint of his apostolate, and it is decisive. It is not Paul who decides, but the decision about him *is made*—and made not by some kind of special enlightenment, but just by the simple fact that for the time being he is still there. To that fact he bows. 'With the true holy ones of God all is genuine human nature' (Horn). Paul would not be Paul if the simple fact that he is still alive, and for example at this very moment sees the Philippians before him, did not point him to the conclusion that he has to do with something *anagkaioteron* (something 'more necessary') to which he has now to submit for a season, whatever his highest hopes one way or another may be.

The hand in which he sees both life and death, and from which he personally looks for death more joyfully than for further life, is the very same hand that appointed him an apostle. And that decides, for the *present* moment conclusively, in favour of 'remaining in the flesh'—namely, and on this the emphasis lies: *for your sakes.*

With that the descent from the precipitous heights of v. 20 is complete. Paul has explained to the Philippians in vv. 21-23 what he meant when he said in v. 18 that whatever happened he would look forward joyfully to what lay before him. He looks forward to it so very much, he has said, that he is tempted actually to wish for the very thing that would mean pain and loss to them, namely, his death—to wish for that more than for the other possibility for which they were hoping. But he requires only to remind himself of the situation, only to think of his apostolate and of them as his congregation, and at once he is right beside them again in their hopes for him. As long as he lives, the *one thing* that makes him what he is, the *one thing* that must determine the attitude he will in fact adopt—they need not fear he will perhaps rush off into martyrdom, for **the thing I count on is:** what is necessary for your sakes. And so **I think I shall remain, remain with you all to your increase and joy in the faith.** The emphasis lies on the last words. Here we detect unmistakably the note of soothing the anxious which Paul manifestly wishes his words to contain— words with which indeed he would free them in principle from all anxiety. *He* comes to rest in the thought of his necessary work *di' hymas* and the *prokopē kai chara tēs pisteōs hymōn* (for your sakes, to your increase and joy in the faith), in the task to which he knows himself bound all along the line so long as he actually *is* bound to it. *They* may rest—he does not begrudge them that—in the *menō kai paramenō* (I remain and shall remain) which is implicitly *also* involved in the necessary work of which *he* is thinking. V. 26 strengthens still further the impression of intentional soothing and comforting. Paul says the aim of his continuing to live is, that they might experience **through him**—that is, in the purely earthly sense, **through my coming to you again**—an **increase of their** *kauchēma*, **glory,** which here no doubt means

concretely: their courage, their confidence, their gratitude and joy-
ousness. That it has to be a case of their **'glory in Christ Jesus'**,
certainly points an admonitory finger here, too, in the different
direction of the apostle's *own* line of thought. We must not fail to
detect the undertone of *reserve* contained even in all the comfort
and promise of this conclusion. Paul as he writes it is doubtless not
thinking quite the same as the Philippians on reading it would at
least *like* to think. He knows he must needs work as long as it is
day. *They* will try above all to take his words to mean that it will
still long be day—which is precisely what Paul only knows con-
ditionally. Looking back over the whole of vv. 12-26, we may
well say that Paul is secretly anxious to induce his readers to think
with him of the one thing needful, the thing that *unconditionally*
can be known and must be known: 'Christ will be magnified!'

CHILDREN OF GOD AMONG A PERVERSE GENERATION

Just one thing: your state must be worthy of the Gospel of Christ, so that when I come and see you, or hear of you from a distance, (I may learn that) you stand (fast) in one Spirit, striving with one soul for the faith of the Gospel, not intimidated even in the least by your adversaries—to them a sign of judgment, but to you of salvation—and that from God. For it is given to you for Christ's sake, not only to believe in him but also to suffer for him, being engaged in the same struggle as you saw in me and now hear of from me. As surely then as admonition in Christ, as surely as encouragement of love, as surely as fellowship of the Spirit, as surely as heartfelt mercy (truly) exist (over you, in you, among you), make my joy complete by minding the one thing, with the one love, one soul, one mind, never by any means assertive or conceited, but in humility one setting the other above himself, each not considering his own point of view but each that of the other. Mind among you that which is minded in Christ Jesus—who being in the form of God did not regard equality with God as spoil, but emptied himself (of that form) and took on the form of a servant, became like men. And being found in his bearing as a man, he humbled himself, became obedient unto death, even to death on the cross. Therefore God has exalted him and given him the name above all names, that in the name of Jesus every knee should bow, of heavenly beings and earthly beings and those under the earth, and every tongue confess: Jesus Christ is Kyrios to the glory of God the Father!—Therefore, my beloved, as indeed you were always obedient, so now work out—not as (something that would happen) only in my presence, but now much more in my absence—with fear and trembling your salvation; for it is God who accomplishes in you both the willing and the accomplishing according to his good pleasure. Do everything without grumbling and cavilling, that you may be blameless and pure, spotless children

**of God in the midst of a perverse and crooked generation,
among whom you shine like the stars in space since you have
the Word of Life**—(and do this) **to my glory against the day of
Christ, that I may not have run in vain nor laboured in vain.**

27-28b. With the *monon*—**Just one thing!**—lifted like a
warning finger, the proviso which in the foregoing was made in
regard to Paul himself only in the form of a mild reserve comes
plainly to light in another form. *Quidquid de me agatur, vos nihilo
minus pergite in recto cursu!* (Whatever may befall *me*, do *you* at all
events continue on the right course!) is Calvin's comment. We
might recall the old Hanseatic motto: *Vivere non necesse est,
navigare necesse est!* (Living is not necessary, but seafaring is!) It
is not the life of Paul that should be *their* care, but the *rectus cursus*,
the *prokopē* (advance) of the Gospel or the faith (vv. 12 and 25), as
far as that can lie in their hands. In embracing 'for your sakes'
(v. 24) his apostolate and with it the 'continuance in the flesh',
Paul also begins anew (not in contrast to his knowledge of the
grace in which the congregation stands but on the ground of his
insight into it, cf. vv. 3-11) his apostolic admonishing, entreating,
adjuring. In order that I too may have my 'glory in Christ' on
your account as you will have on mine, v. 26 (so the thought here
has no doubt to be expanded from the end of the paragraph, 2.16)
namely, when it comes to what you are hoping for and what I
accordingly hope for with you—**when I come and see you, or
hear of you from a distance**[1]—then a condition must be fulfilled on your side. You must be in a **state,**[2] a *politeuesthai*,
worthy of the Gospel of Christ.[3] The word *politeuesthai* which
Paul here uses instead of *peripatein*, with which it is largely
synonymous in the *Koinē*,[4] recalls that kingdom established in

---

[1] The sentence is curtailed, and the connecting verb is missing.
[2] There is a certain play on the fact that the German word (*Verfassung*) can
mean both '(political) constitution' and also 'frame of mind', 'attitude', etc.
(*Translator*).
[3] It seems to me in view of 3.20 impossible to approve Lueken's translation:
'Conduct your congregational life in such a way as . . .', and Schlatter's: 'Ad-
minister the congregation in such a way as. . . .'.
[4] Cf. Dibelius on this passage.

heaven, of which Christians here on earth, amid the homeless anarchy of this aeon, are secretly now already citizens (3.20). Their state, their 'form', their bearing must therefore here and now already be under the invisible discipline of that kingdom, must in fact be in accordance with *the* 'state' which is to be reflected in their conduct, 'worthy' of the Gospel, the gracious message which in Christ was issued to them and received by them concerning that kingdom. That it is impossible to deduce from this state 'worthy' of the Gospel any special 'worth' of the men so constituted, follows not only from the infinite distance that will always exist in principle between them and the heavenly prototype of their state, but also from the very nature of the case, from the fact that it is a question of being worthy of *grace*. 'To live from grace oneself and impute grace to one's neighbour is what it means to be a citizen of the kingdom of God' (Horn). The depravity of those who are 'worthy' in the sense of this passage is not denied by *this* kind of worth, but rather asserted.

The fundamental principle of this state in which Paul would have the Philippians to be is plainly to be sought in the main verb, **that you stand,** on which the participial clauses that follow depend, and to which the relative clause v. 28b is related back. They are to stand **fast**—that is the meaning. For, as is plain from vv. 28-30, they are being troubled, are in danger of being shaken; they have adversaries, they have to suffer, they are engaged in a struggle. 'Worthy' in v. 27 means *in concreto*: firm, manly, showing backbone, confessing—whereby the Gospel is conceived as the ground on which they are to maintain their stand, from which they are not to let themselves be forced away (cf. e.g. I Cor. 15.1; II Cor. 1.24). Everything in vv. 27-30 revolves round that, and the end of the paragraph (2.15-16) will return to the same note. And therein lies the inner connexion between vv. 27-30 and the preceding paragraph vv. 12-26, especially vv. 21-26. Paul makes it also outwardly plain in v. 30. He is engaged in a struggle in Rome. In their concern as to how he is faring in it, they are not by any means to forget (he has told them tacitly what *his* 'state' is in *his* struggle!) to stand fast in their *own* struggle. This is the thread on which the individual thoughts must now be strung.

They are to stand fast **in one Spirit.** In view of the parallels to
histanai en it will not be advisable to make any distinction between
this *pneuma* (spirit) and the Holy Spirit of God and of Christ. At
all events it denotes that immediacy in their standing to God
which they *have received*. It is by continuing to stand before God
on the ground thus jointly *received* that they are to stand fast.[1] Paul
adds, perhaps already in view of the following *synathlountes* (striving): **with one soul.** *This* unity at any rate is certainly derived,
secondary. The 'soul' is the spiritual part of man in itself. Unity
in the 'Spirit' is no task (*Aufgabe*), but a gift (*Gabe*) that men need
only call to mind again in order to be united. Unity of 'souls' is a
task. Bengel, who knew what people are, makes the remark: *est
interdum inter sanctos naturalis aliqua antipathia*! (There is at times
even among the holy a kind of natural antipathy). Where the
'antipathies' of soul are not got rid of, there the contemplation of
the 'unity in the Spirit' has manifestly not yet taken place, and
then there cannot be much of the joint standing fast against joint
difficulties either.

The Christians are to **strive for the faith of the Gospel.** Thus
Paul does not say: *against* the adversaries later mentioned. That
would be typical of the later—and present-day—situation, in
which Christians stood and stand as a party against other parties
(e.g. against 'Rome', against 'modern unbelief', etc.). This situation is thoroughly corrupt. Christians do not strive 'against' anybody (nor *for* anybody either!), but *for the faith*. Pertinence and
victory in that struggle depend on the observance of this distinction! The struggle which Paul means can be fought in earnest
only against oneself. Not even for one's own faith! *Pistis tou
euangeliou* (faith of the Gospel) is subjective genitive! 'Faith is not
mine but God's. If I struggle for my faith, then I do not know
what I am striving after, nor even whether it is lasting and worth
while. If I struggle for God's faithfulness, then I slay Goliath'
(Horn).

Who the **adversaries** mentioned in v. 28 were, we do not
know. To think of the false teachers mentioned in 3.2 does not

[1] The very last thing Lueken should have done was to translate: 'borne up by
one enthusiasm (*Begeisterung*)'.

seem appropriate, since here it is manifestly not a question of seducers of the congregation but of opponents. And in this context they have no interest in themselves. That the Christians are not to let themselves be **intimidated,** impressed, disconcerted by them, **not even in the least,** making no concessions, not even the smallest, that they are to conform entirely to their own basic principle, which they have not chosen for themselves but which has chosen them, without looking to right or left—that is what Paul understands by 'standing fast'. This fact, he goes on, that you stand fast—one in Spirit and in soul as you strive for the faith without letting yourselves be led astray even in the very least— this fact is *sufficient*. He does not promise the Philippians that they will triumph and their opponents be defeated. But he tells them: this fact will be set up as a **sign,** an indication, a testimony, a declaration. It will, however things turn out, speak for itself— namely, of the **destruction,** of the eternal judgment under which those who reject the 'faith of the Gospel' stand here and now already in the shadow of the coming day of God, *and* of the **salvation** which in the light of the same day is here and now accomplished in those who assent to that faith. This sign requires to be set up 'in the midst of a perverse and crooked generation, among whom you shine like the stars in space' (2.15). *To that end* the Christians are to 'stand fast', and it is in that that they are to see their 'worth'. The proclamation of the menace and promise of the Kingdom of God must not cease. That is what Christians are set in society for. They guarantee it by their existence.

28c-30.   And that from God! is added at once. Let there be no misunderstanding! 'Because you have the Word of Life', is given in 2.16 as the ground of the great promise to Christians as 'children of God'. It is not *you* who set up this sign in the world, this lighthouse that sends out beams of light on all sides, but leaves also broad belts of darkness in between and makes them appear all the darker: 'to the one a savour of life unto life, to the other a savour of death unto death' (II Cor. 2.16) *kai touto apo theou* (and that of God). Because God is concerned for *his* cause and *therefore* for you, because by 'standing fast' you give yourselves up to

him, commit yourselves for good or ill into his hands—therefore
and thereby you create truth in the world, judging and pardoning
truth of God. Notice once again: Paul says no more of the Christians' struggle in the world than that thereby a 'sign' (*endeixis*) of
destruction and of deliverance is set up. They are to rest content
with that. He promises victory to *them* just as little as he set before
them the prospect of a happy turn to his own affliction. 'Our *faith*
is the victory that overcomes the world', I John 5.4. 'Our faith'
—that is never and under no circumstances *ourselves*! The grace
of which he says in v. 29 that it has already been **given** them is
rather the grace **not only to believe in Christ but also to suffer
for him,** in exact parallel to v. 7 and v. 21. The grace of being
permitted to *believe* in Christ is surpassed by the grace of being
permitted to *suffer* for him, of being permitted to walk the way of
Christ with Christ himself to the perfection of fellowship with
him. That is where standing fast, being one and striving for the
faith leads: truly not to a Christian triumph, but to a Christian
defeat. It is in the midst of that defeat, and not apart from it, that
the 'sign' is set up. But it is grace, it is God's gift, that one is thus
used as a *sacrifice* (Paul will say this of himself in the next section,
2.17), permitted to get the worst of it that God may have the
glory of it. To perceive that, to assent to it, is what the 'state'
worthy of the Gospel (v. 27) ultimately comes to.

On v. 30 my whole exegesis of the preceding verses and the
preceding section (vv. 12-26) has been constructed. I therefore
hardly need to make any further special comment on it.

Let us look first of all summarily at the next verses, **2.1-11,** as
they form a more closely co-ordinated whole within the framework of our paragraph. A text like this can hardly be approached
with sufficient care and concentration. For it offers so much in so
few verses—a little compendium of Pauline testimony. Everything is here conjoined and interwoven. First something *personal*:
that inimitable Pauline solicitation, prayer and entreaty with
which the apostle so to speak importunes his readers, yet without
thereby losing his authority even for a moment. Then the heart
of the Pauline *ethic* (cf. Rom. 12.3 ff.), where seemingly so little,

but in fact everything, is demanded by saying that each is to climb down from the throne on which he sits, and to mind and seek after the *one* end, which is then also that of the *others* and in which all *must* find their way to unity. And then—where is the boundary here between 'ethics' and 'dogmatics'? there should indeed be none, one is nothing if it is not also the other—then the great comparison between this mind that climbs down in order to direct itself to the one end and 'minding that which is minded *in Christ Jesus*'. The law that was just laid down has of course been fulfilled, the Christians can only take their *start* from that fulfilment: for what must happen among them *has* already happened. That 'unity in the Spirit' is no ideal: it is there, it is given in the fellowship of those who are 'in Christ Jesus'. To be mindful of that unity and let it consummate itself is the only thing to which the 'minding' just demanded can be directed. Then the extraordinarily rich expansion of this fact, the disclosure of the *presuppositions* of the unity as the congregation reminds itself of them in calling Jesus Christ the Lord. How does he come to be the Lord? What are the consequences for those who call *him* their Lord? There now follows in broad lines a picture of his passage from heaven via the earth back to heaven—and not for a moment does the solicitation, prayer and entreaty thereby cease, not for a moment can or should the little concrete step thereby be forgotten which Paul wishes of his readers: that each should humble himself—yes, *should*, precisely *because* in Christ Jesus there is no 'should' but only being and consummation.

And hence also here, at least for *us*, the riddle of the origin of the whole. What is the primary thing, the really vital point in these verses?—the *personal* (psychological!) aspect, Paul and the Philippians, the Philippians and Paul?—or that *ethic* that can never become morals, that moves like a spinning top only on its point, nowhere impinges, nowhere calls a halt, and yet remains truly ethic, law, inexorable demand?—or the *background* that suddenly opens up in vv. 5 ff., the great story of the movement in God and from God towards man, which to Paul and his readers is apparently anything but dry metaphysics, which they do not by any means stand impartially contemplating, but are involved in

the midst of it 'in Christ Jesus'? Or is in fact nothing here primary
and nothing derivative? Are these not three really distinguishable
circles at all, but all beginning, all middle, all end—are the
'psychological', the 'ethical' *and* the 'dogmatic' one single Reality
whose evidences we have here before us? Must *everything* be clear
to us here, unless we prefer to confess that *everything* is here
obscure to us? At all events, one would almost like to say: why
tear it all to pieces in explanation? Those who understand it surely
understand it without any explanation? Yet the task is given us,
here as much as anywhere else. Except that here more than ever
we set about it with the proviso that all explaining can only be
assisting the *text* to explain itself. That has to be said in a *different*
sense of the Bible than of other books, and of a text such as this
more than of other Bible texts.

The connexion with what precedes is as close and simple as it
could be. The *admonition* to the Philippians which had begun in
1.27 continues. *One* definite demand now becomes central: the
realization of the fellowship, of the unity of Christians among
themselves. The thought does not appear for the first time. When
he first began to explain the word 'stand' which dominates vv.
27-30—i.e. by adding in *one* Spirit, with *one* soul (v. 27)—Paul
had already been aiming that way. It is obviously *this* that is
specially at stake in the struggle for the faith, in the setting up of
the 'sign'. One can take 2.1-11 as an excursus on these words.

**1. As surely then as admonition in Christ, as surely as
encouragement of love, as surely as fellowship of the
Spirit, as surely as heartfelt mercy** truly exists—so Paul turns
to his readers, visibly making a completely new start. The meaning of the verse is in general plain. Paul wishes to say: if in anything I have your hearts, your ears, access to you as an apostle,
then you must hear me in what I am now going to say. The
urgency of this opening is the more striking when one considers
how far Paul in fact already presupposed that he had such access
to *these* readers. Here it seems as if he would after all put a new
question mark to all his presuppositions in that respect. There is a
certain all too great accessibility and openness, for which words
that are meant in a fundamental sense can no longer be heard as

CANISIUS COLLEGE LIBRARY
BUFFALO, N. Y.

such. And then sometimes a *loud* summons is necessary: Do you really *hear*, my dear, willing, open-minded hearers? It will be well to understand all four parts of the verse as descriptions of the access, the open inner road between Paul and the Philippians, and not divide them in some such way as to make the first two refer to what can happen from Paul's side, the last two to what is to be expected of the Philippians. 'Exhortation in Christ' could truly be described as the category of thought under which 'moral' encouragement becomes possible and necessary with Paul. Ethics with a Pauline orientation could bear no other title than that. Paul means: as surely as it is possible and necessary for you to be admonished (=comforted!) in Christ. With the 'encouragement of love' we shall have to think in the context of these verses likewise of the love of Christ, which according to II Cor. 5.14 *synechei* (binds) Paul, so that whether he be considered a wise man for it or a fool, he is constrained to speak in this way and no other. The 'fellowship of the Spirit' describes the ultimate bond between the writer and the addressees as also between the addressees themselves, to which he wishes to appeal, thus the *terminus a quo* and the *terminus ad quem* (the starting-point and goal) of what he has to say. Finally 'heartfelt mercy' according to the parallel in Rom. 12.1 will likewise have to be understood as a description of the reason that lies in God's ways, for the attitude demanded of them, or rather, for the demand itself: as surely as God has with all his heart shown mercy to you.[1]

2. Make my joy complete—it now comes more plainly to light than in the first chapter what Paul misses even in the Philippian

---

[1] Some difficulty is caused by the grammatically troublesome *tis* at the beginning of these last phrases. Hofmann let it mislead him into the following interpretation of the verse: *if* there be admonition, then let it be admonition in Christ, *if* encouragement, then let it be loving encouragement, *if* spiritual fellowship, yes *if* any (the fateful *tis* would thus belong to the third phrase as intensification), then let it be affection and mercy! It is nowadays supposed that this is a case of the use of an indeclinable *tis*—whereby of course the *ei ti* in the second phrase becomes a puzzle, so that the supposition has to be resorted to that the fateful *s* has there dropped out. A doubt consequently *remains*. At all events the manifold *tis* serves to sharpen the urgency with which Paul wishes to speak.

congregation—**by minding the one thing.** We have before us here the New Testament idea in which Schleiermacher especially as a preacher thought to rediscover his own deepest insights. 'Mind the one thing!' The expression occurs also in Rom. 12.16; 15.5, and will recur in 4.7. We do not know in Philippians what gave concrete occasion for this admonition. We hear nothing at any rate of divisions of a material kind such as we know of from Romans and I Corinthians. According to a rather unkind exposition it was the two women mentioned in 4.2, Euodia and Syntyche, who had brought discord into the congregation. Be that as it may. In view of the striking fact that the admonition to preserve peace and fellowship is a largely stereotype one that appears somewhere in almost all the New Testament Epistles, it will be best to be clear that a 'movement' such as these congregations were engaged in had also, at least transitionally, a strongly centrifugal action. It is not the case that men at once come to a better understanding among themselves also, the better they understand God. First of all, perhaps, it will be rather the contrary: each individual is then powerfully forced back on himself, discovers himself before God as an *individual* as opposed to common humanity in general. It means a second, separate step when he goes on from that to the knowledge of the *unity* of God's congregation and to the *will* to embrace this *una sancta* (this 'one holy [Church]') Perhaps those who do not know the first do not know what the second means. But this second step *must* come. The opposition of the individual to fellowship in God can really only rest on the fact that the individual does not yet understand himself rightly either.

'Mind the one thing', *to auto*.[1] This command must first of all be allowed to stand in all its generality. It is not for that reason empty of content. For indeed it is very pregnant with meaning— and the meaning is, *the* one thing beside which there is no other. The 'one thing' is at all events no human truth and righteousness,

[1] It should be noted that the German (like the Greek) says simply 'the one', without specifying whether the noun to be supplied is 'end', 'principle', 'Object', or what. Thus even 'thing', though necessary in English, means a certain narrowing of the expression which, in itself, is wholly indefinite, entirely general (*Translator*).

not mine, yours, his. Nor is it the sum of the kinds of human truth and righteousness united in the fellowship, between which some sort of tolerance would then have to be exercised. But it is, as later emerges, the divine Source of everything that can be truth and righteousness to *these* individuals. This divine Source sets the limit to the centrifugal action to which the individuals are at first submitted. Those who look to it as the 'one thing' see that limit and begin to respect it. It is to be supposed, although the concrete details are all hidden from us, that it was also in Philippi a case of radical disunity. Against purely personal squabbles Paul would perhaps hardly have marshalled the powerful array that now follows. That the people of Philippi are not even yet *so* serious as to put the seriousness of the *one* thing *above* the seriousness with which each regards *himself*, is what Paul misses to make his 'joy' in the congregation complete. Paul, too, thinks radically, but he sees further (1.18 f.): there is one *ultimate* radical thing which no individual can play off against *others* as his own radicalness, but which rather takes the field for and against each individual, and has at all times the purpose of putting an end to even the most radical dispute.

It is in recollection of *that*, of the 'one thing', that he goes on to say: **with the one love, one soul, one mind.** In recollection of *that*, this *can* be said, and is no moral triviality, no airy demand for a splendid impossibility. The first expression, *tēn autēn agapēn echontes* (with the one love), portrays so to speak how *to auto* (the one thing), which the many, the individuals, the hermits know well enough, enters as *hē autē* (the same) into their relationship with each other. This relationship must of course be 'love', and yet it is such weak, human, limited love so long and so far as the marrow of the 'one thing' is missing—as also the 'one thing' is not the 'one thing' at all so long and so far as each individual thinks he can somehow have it for himself, so long and so far as it has not entered into their relationship to each other. *To auto* (the one thing) and the *agapē* (love) must find each other, Paul means. That will also be what is meant by becoming 'one soul' which recalls the expression *mia psychē* (with one soul) in 1.27. The 'souls'—it can of course after all only be the 'souls' that quarrel—

are brought as it were under a common yoke, and must pull together the same plough. That is the 'bond of peace' (Eph. 4.3), the only thing that can unite really seriously disunited souls, but that *can* and *must* unite them. 'One mind' seems to indicate the purpose. *To hen* (one [mind]) is not the same as *to auto* (the one thing). *To auto* is more comprehensive, it is objective, qualitative: the one thing on which the mind must be set because it is the unique thing, different in kind from everything human, the thing that makes a claim on the disunited simply by its *worth*. *To hen* on the other hand is that which is common, which unites, brings together and binds together. Only by the roundabout route via *to auto* is there any point in speaking of *to hen*, but then there *is* point in it. Whoever minds the *one* thing, minds also the common thing. Objectivity—but then of course the objectivity that means the absoluteness of the Object—is in all cases the way to peace. But Paul becomes still more specific.

3. Never by any means assertive or conceited. Meyer's translation is surely on the crude side: 'cliquish or braggartlike' (*kabalenmässig oder renomistisch*). The case is a more subtle one. *Eritheia* denotes properly the behaviour of a man who insists on his wages, who wants to be paid, then of course more generally: the ways, straight or crooked, by which a man seeks to promote his cause, his advantage. Since the process here surely lies in the spiritual realm, 'assertive'[1] will be the appropriate translation. *Kenodoxia* is decking oneself out with an appearance that has nothing behind it, or at least not what corresponds to the appearance. What Paul is seeking to describe are two nuances of the same attitude. Where does assertiveness end, where does conceit begin? Both together describe the bearing of a man who indeed but a moment ago *was* in fact in the right, perhaps also on the point in dispute—and now it is suddenly after all only the human all-too-human element that shows up in him: the zealous man has turned into a zealot, the fighter into a wrangler. Either his perception or his honesty stands in doubt, or even both. It can happen that way! That is the one way it must *not* happen, says

[1] *Rechthaberisch* describes literally, the man who 'is always right' (*Translator*).

Paul, interpreting his *hina to auto phronēte* (mind the one thing) first of all in a negative sense. This all-too-human element *could* be behind the inability of the Philippian Christians to be united, however serious the grounds of their disunity might be. It would be worth while to reflect on this possibility. Notice that the verb is missing—perhaps intentionally, otherwise *phronountes, legontes, poiountes,* or the like would have to be supplied. Minding the 'one thing' would necessarily bring it to light if it were in fact this very ordinary human failing that was disturbing the peace. And where indeed would this very ordinary failing have no say in the matter at all?

The next words bring the positive elucidation: **but in humility one setting the other above himself.** We must not try to whittle that down. It does not say: each should look around for good qualities in the other, in which that other could perhaps be superior to him, *licet praestantiorem se noverit* (although for the rest he considers himself better). Calvin interpreted it that way. But that will not do. At that rate a man could go on occupying unmolested the castle he occupies. No, Paul now gives his *to auto* a positive turn. He takes it for granted that in face of the 'one thing' there can be room only for humility. But, he says, really to set our mind on the 'one thing' means to adopt a completely new attitude to our neighbour. Humility in face of the 'one thing' now becomes practical, relevant. The 'one thing' is after all—and that is why it calls for humility—the judging grace under which the congregation stands. To believe in grace means concretely: to set the other above oneself. My neighbour is its bearer and representative, and therefore in comparison with me a *hyperechōn* (a superior). Which neighbour? The good, clever, earnest, pious one, to whom I willingly bow as such? No, the word *hyperechontas* recalls the *exousiai hyperechousai* of Rom. 13.1, the authorities that have *power without regard to* their quality. And it says simply *allēlous* (one another) without restriction. This *hēgeisthai* (setting [above oneself]) is a case of an *a priori*, not of an *a posteriori*. The dispute ends when we discover respect for each other, not on this ground or that, perhaps *without* any grounds, *counter* to every ground, simply because we are bidden when looking at our neighbour to think of the 'one thing', of grace—to see him, in his foolishness and wickedness it may be, as a messenger of its sovereignty. Grace certainly does not live and move abstractly, nor transcendently: it comes to meet us in life, in the efforts, hopes, insights, concerns of those about me, in whose company I stand before God as an individual, by whom indeed I am set before God as an individual. The strange, different, unintelligible subjective aspect of my neighbour is the garment in which the *one thing* meets me. The claim my neighbour makes on me—on my patience, attention, consideration, on my love—is the claim of the *one thing*. The confused voice I hear out there, often so unattractive, so contrary to my own subjective outlook, is the voice of the *one thing*. The disturbance on my island, which every neighbour first of all means for me, is disturbance by the *one thing* that I keep forgetting. We do not think that way, but that is how we *must* think, says Paul. Humility in face of the 'one thing' is genuine when it is the humility in which we think *that way of each other*. Humility *in abstracto* can be the grossest pride. Seeking the 'one thing' in heaven can mean not seeking it at all. In humility let each consider the *other* higher than himself. This practical version of humility before God has nothing to do with any feeble self-surrender, with illusions about men, and such like. In this humility the head can and should be held high. In it we can and should know what men are. It is to the *grace* in man that the respect is paid. That respect is the foundation of the fellowship in the congregation. All *other* kinds of consideration, obligingness, understanding and such like provide *no* foundation for fellowship. The *one* thing must be on the field if it is to come to the *to hen phronein* (being of one mind). Paul brings it on the field by setting our neighbour before us as our *hyperechōn* (our superior).

4 formulates the same thought once again: **each not considering his own point of view[1] but that of the others.** In the Greek here the *kai* in the second half of the sentence is perplexing. The

---

[1] 'Point of view' must here be taken in the widest possible sense: the German (and Greek) have simply 'his own', which can include anything and everything that is vitally related to him (*Translator*).

edge would be taken off the argument if it were really to be translated: *also* that of the others. The note of absoluteness which was
struck by the *hyperechontas* of v. 3, and which will presently sound
again in a very different form, would be remarkably weakened
thereby.[1] Obviously we have again to do with that untranslatable
kai that is meant to serve only to emphasize what follows. Then
the whole forms a parallel to v. 3b and a closer definition of it.
Those whose attitude Paul is here objecting to 'see', notice or
consider in all they see *ta heautōn* (their own), as those mentioned
in 2.21 seek their own. Everything at once takes on the colour of
their own personality. They take it for granted that everything is
there in order to be seen from their particular standpoint. They
drag everything into the sphere of their own wishes, viewpoints
and concerns. Everything is to be grist to their mill. In all the
things Paul is referring to here, we shall do well not to think at
once of ordinary, common self-seeking, but rather of processes,
conflicts and errors of a subtle, spiritual, religious kind. If we are
reaching too high in that, then we can console ourselves with the
thought that common selfishness is included in what is said of
the subtler kind. The contrary would not be the case. Well, then:
they are not only sitting each on his own island, but on that
island each also on his own *throne*. *That* is why disunity is inevi-
table, even without any particular quarrelsomeness on their part:
simply as a result of the ideal heights on which each has established
himself. To climb down from that throne is the way to peace—
to consider the others' point of view. That here again the others
are not just simply the other people in general who have *also* a
will to live, who should *also* be allowed *something* without a
grudge, who should *also* be considered, can be learned from a
glance at 2.21, where the place of the 'others' is taken by—Christ
himself. The *heteroi* (others) are the *allēloi* (those comprised by the
words 'each other') of v. 3, the bearers of grace, and as such—and
that is why we should not consider our own point of view but

---

[1] Even if we were to adopt Hofmann's interpretation: the first, negative half
of the sentence forbids each individual for himself to be intent only on his own
advantage, the second, positive half commands each individual on his part to
make his aim the best interest also of others.

theirs—the representatives of a higher Authority. The reason why we are to see the other's point of view, to let ourselves be enticed out of our own hut and over into his, is not that that were supposedly a holy place, but that it is only when men thus come *together*, when they take a *joint* view of things, when they bow *jointly* before him who is greater than both my neighbour and myself—it is only then that the really holy, true and helpful One comes into my field of vision at all. It is not until I see the other's point of view that I myself really see. By means of others' thoughts I learn to think thoughts of my own. By giving freedom I am free. By obeying I exercise myself in governing. Always my neighbour is the barrier, but also the door. There is no road that passes him by.

With v. 5 the imperious *hina to auto phronēte* (mind the one thing) is suddenly given a different guise. It does not lose its seriousness and its sharpness. But it now becomes clear where the absolute tone that was adopted comes from—clear that it is no ideology that is at stake when Paul bids his readers 'mind the one thing', and that they must understand him immediately when he points to such a seemingly empty cipher. Now we are given to see the Reality in which it has all been said, the Reality in which the disputants who are to accept the admonition exist, the Reality in which men *can* and *must* be pointed to their neighbour, to the other and to the other's point of view. **Mind among you that which must be minded in Christ Jesus.** For that is how the verb missing at the end of the sentence must be supplied: *ho en Christō Iēsou phronein dei*. Not something like: *ho en Christō Iēsou ephrōnēthē* or *ēn*. In other words not: 'let each be so minded as Jesus Christ also was'. It is not by a reference to the *example* of Christ that Paul would strengthen what was said in vv. 1-4, but by equating the 'minding' there spoken of with *the* 'minding' that is commanded, that is our self-evident task, within the *order* designated by the formula *en Christō Iēsou* (in Christ Jesus). Again the *kai* emphasizes the sentence's leading idea in the words that follow it. *En Christō Iēsou* designates in point of fact the reality, the place, the area in which the people addressed exist. They exist in the *fellowship* of Christ Jesus, they are members of his *body.* Set your minds, Paul means to say, on the truth (and on its natural implications for conscience and will) which is manifested and apprehended in the place where *you* stand. For indeed the place where Paul's readers (and Paul himself with them) find themselves differs from other places in that in it truth of a quite definite kind continually presents itself for apprehension and is in fact apprehended. The grace of God in Christ Jesus is the place in question, and the truth that there presents itself for apprehension and is in fact apprehended is that law that does not wait to be somehow recognized and put into force but in this place is naturally and inalienably valid and constantly puts itself into force—the law of *grace.* The *touto phroneite* (mind that which . . .) of this verse is obviously a commentary on the *hina to auto phronēte* (that you mind *the one thing*) of v. 2, and proves that we do well there already to shun all explanations of a colourless, philosophical kind. There already, as here becomes plain, what is meant by the object on which the Christian mind is set is *this*—that men *en Christō Iēsou* stand in the light of that quite definite truth and are subject to the law of grace.

What now stands in vv. 6 ff. must be understood as if Paul suddenly lifted a curtain or opened a door: the topic becomes the Reality itself, in which Paul speaks and the Philippians hear. For a moment the background against which the conversation takes place is brought into view and given plasticity and perspective. We now know where and how the sort of things can be said that are said in 1.27-2.4. The Reality which is constitutive of the Church, and within which the law is in force, is summed up in its Head, *Christ Jesus.* To contemplate his way is immediately, without any special application being necessary, to contemplate the *law* that operates in his Church. Paul has no need to revert to the *to auto phronein* (mind the one thing) of v. 2 after this pointer has been given to the background, to the object of the only *phronein* (minding) that is possible in the Church. Let us now try to follow his pointer.

6. The Christ **who being in the form of God did not regard equality with God as spoil.** That is he by whom the Church is

founded and ruled, in whom it is summed up as in its Head. In
order to understand here, we must start from the *to einai isa theō*
(the being equal with God). He is '*equal with God*'. That is the
beginning of the way we are to be shown. It will also (vv. 9-11)
be the end of it—for the Bearer of the 'name above all names',
in whose name every knee bows, who is confessed by every
tongue as *Kyrios*, is obviously no less (or in what should the 'less'
consist?) than he who is there designated as *theos patēr* (God the
Father) and the One to whose glory it all happens. This equality
of Christ with God is so to speak the fixed, *ultimate* background,
from which his road sets out and to which it returns. Paul has not
developed the lines that would have to be developed in order to
make the co-existence of God the Father and Christ intelligible.
For himself and his readers the relationship in question was intelligible in itself. We shall not go into that here either. The question
whether such co-existence might not mean a threat to mono-
theism is at all events one that need not trouble us. Vv. 10-11 show
that Paul, in spite of this co-existence or rather in the form of this
co-existence, sees all the threads of the world's life come together
in one hand—and that with a consistency that could stand in very
sharp contrast to that of many a supposedly purer monotheist.
Yet it is not of Christ's equality with God that our passage would
speak, but of what Christ, acting as God's Equal, is, does and
means.

The first decisive statement: this, his own most proper, so to
speak natural being, his equality with God, he **did not regard as
spoil.** We must think back to vv. 3 and 4, to the Christians who
think, live and 'seek their own' *kat' eritheian* (assertively) and *kata
kenodoxian* (conceitedly). *Harpagmon hēgeisthai* (to regard as spoil)
is a stronger expression for the same thing. Christ too has an
'own', he too could assert his rights, he too could pride himself on
his *doxa* (glory), with immeasurably more cause than we. The
thing that is 'his own' is in fact his equality with God. He could
lay hold on that and assert and defend his property as a robber does
his spoil. That is the meaning of *harpagmon hēgeisthai*: to cling
tooth and nail to something. Some have recalled here the myths
about rebellious angels or spirits who were bent on being equal

with God. But in vv. 3-4, which provide the proper standard of comparison here, we have nothing analogous to rebellion of that sort, but only wholly naïve, legitimate self-assertion on the part of individual Christians among themselves. Paul sets over against that the fact that Christ does not make any such '*noli me tangere*' out of his equality with God. He has no need to, because he is *sure* of his *being* equal with God. It is for that very reason that he can also empty himself of the '*form* of God', as it is presently put. 'He *was* in the form of God.' The expression therefore does not denote the same as 'equality with God'. *En morphē theou hyparchein* means to be God in outward appearance, immediately and directly knowable as such. Christ *is* God like that. Nothing prevents his being so *only* like that, *mutatis mutandis* like the people of Philippi who certainly not only are what they are but would also like to be seen for what they are, each in his own right, with his own point of view, with his own value which, in order to be value, of course seeks also outward credit. But now, says Paul, Christ does not regard his equality with God in such a way as to cling to the *form* of God, or be bound to it. He is so much God's Equal that he does not by any means have to make of his equality with God a thing to be asserted tooth and nail—not because he could also give it up, but because his possession of it (in contrast to the best that they can possess) is beyond dispute. When we are absolutely sure of a thing, we have no need to lay hold on it in the robber-like fashion described. To the extent to which two lovers, for example, really belong to each other, they can also give themselves freely, without fear of losing themselves. So too the Son of God certainly does not give away his equality with God, does not give it up, but he does *let go* of it.[1] From now on he is equal with God in the obscurity of the form of a servant. He is *in humility* the highest. The robber-like bearing, the half-anxious, half-greedy graspingness, the assertiveness and vanity of those in Philippi betrays the uncertainty of their possession. Christ, *being* equal with God, has no need to assert himself in that or to

---

[1] There is a play on the words *frei geben* (given freely), *preisgeben* (give away), *aufgeben* (give up) and *freigeben* (let go). It could perhaps be retained by rendering the last one 'giv ʰeave' (*Translator*).

cling to it, but can renounce the outward appearance and credit that correspond to such being, without surrendering the being itself—indeed, in order precisely *thereby* (vv. 9 ff.) to bring it into credit.

That is what he actually does, that is his *way*, the description of which now follows: **He emptied himself** (of that form) **and took on the form of a servant, became like men.** Notice the initial *heauton* (himself). It is thus no fate that overtakes him. Not even the will of the Father is mentioned as the ground of his performing this act of renunciation. He *wills* it so. In sovereign, divine freedom he puts off the form of God, the whole knowability of his being—that is what *ekenōse* means, thus not only that he concealed it. He puts himself in a position where only he himself knows himself in the way that the Father knows him. In the unknowability into which he enters, it is now certainly the Father's part to reveal him. But the step that brings him into that unrecognizable condition, into the *incognito*, is grounded entirely in himself alone. That is how he takes on the 'form of a servant', the appearance and the credit (or rather lack of credit) of a being that is not God, that is not the Lord. (The expression surely looks forward to the radiant *kyrios Iēsous Christos*, 'Jesus Christ is Kyrios', of v. 11.) He comes to 'exist in the image of man' (we recall by way of explanation the *sarx egeneto*, 'and the Word became flesh', of John 1.14, and the still sharper Pauline parallel in Rom. 8.3: *en homoiōmati sarkos hamartias*, 'in the form of *sin-dominated* flesh'!). That means: he exists in such a way that to any direct, immediate way of regarding him—e.g. to the historical and psychological approach—he does not present the picture of his proper, original, divine Being, but solely the picture of a human being. That is the way it is now with the heavenly Head of the Church. That is how Christ asserts and defends his honour. That is how he strives for recognition. That is how he establishes his rights. Is he not equal with God? He is. But where, then, do we see any sign of that? Where is the glittering crown of his Godhead? The *humilitas carnis* (humility of the flesh) covers the *divina majestas* (divine majesty) like a curtain, says Calvin. It does so all along the line. There must be no turning and twisting of the

ekenōse (emptied) and the *homoiōma* (like [men]). The second
term, too, stresses the likeness, and not in some way the hidden
unlikeness. What we see is a man, the form of one exposed to all
the dubiousness, ambiguity and darkness of an individual human
existence, the form not of a lord but of a servant. He emptied
himself of the form of God in taking on our form. It is God's
Equal himself, in all his freedom and his entirely royal sovereignty,
who is the ground of this *incognito*. We must surely therefore
abstain from seeking to penetrate it. The will of God himself
would oppose us if we did. Flesh and blood cannot, may not and
will not reveal to us who this is. It is precisely as such—as he who
emptied himself, as he who became a man without reduction or
addition—that he is the Head of the Church. How should he be
that in any other way? In view of vv. 3-4 the inference follows of
itself.

But Paul is not yet finished: **Being found in his bearing as a
man, he humbled himself, became obedient unto death,
even to death on the cross.** These words form to a certain extent
a contrast to the preceding. God's Equal forgoes asserting himself
as such, enters into the obscurity of human nature, seeks not to be
called good (Mark 10.18) but like all other men to live by grace.
That is the first statement. Now the second: having thus become
like men and been found to bear himself as a man, he takes in
that capacity the same step into the depths once again. He in
whom no one will seek or find God's Equal—he does not even
assume some *pinnacle* of the human scene. Once more he does not
stand where the people of Philippi apparently stand—not where
the battle is fought for honour, right and credit—but: he humbled
himself. We think of the *tapeinophrosynē* (humility) of v. 3. Once
again: he humbled *himself*. Kierkegaard[1] has left us the following
note on this passage: 'Christ humbled *himself*—not, he *was*
humbled. O infinite sublimity, of which it must categorically be
true that there was none in heaven or on earth or in the abyss
that could humble him! He humbled himself. The infinite qualitative difference between Christ and every other man lies indeed in
this, that in every humiliation which he suffers it is absolutely

[1] *Tagebücher*, ed. Haecker II, 122.

necessary that he himself should assent and confirm that he is willing to submit to that humiliation. This is infinite superiority over suffering, but at the same time also suffering infinitely more intense in kind.'

'He became obedient unto death.' Paul, if the passage is read in its context, is not concerned as to *whom* Christ obeyed in his self-humiliation as a man, in his climbing down even from every human pedestal. He is interested rather in the fact *that* he obeys, in the attitude of submission and dependence he adopts. 'He became obedient' looks back to the assumption of the form of a servant in v. 7, and to that extent—but only to that extent—forwards to the proclamation of the *kyriotēs* (the 'Kyrios-glory') in v. 11. It denotes in the most thoroughgoing way the direct opposite of all Kyrios-glory—hence of all things not, as Schleiermacher in almost all his Good Friday sermons used to explain it, the consummate union of Christ with the Father, but precisely the consummation of *that* aspect of God's Equal which puts his equality with God and his unity with the Father wholly in doubt. Despite the fact that this, God's Equal, was found as nothing but an obedient slave, he *was* God's Equal and was recognized and confirmed by God as such—because of the humiliation of God's Equal that went the length of such obedience, not because of the moral achievement of this Man. The humiliation which corresponds to the self-emptying of God's Equal now that he has become man's equal, went the length of *death*. That is its *second*-last step. That it went 'even to death on the *cross*', the *criminal's* death, is its last and lowest one. Vv. 7 and 8 are best understood not as a continuous series, but as two parallels drawn at different levels and describing basically the same process. What happens to the Man Jesus in his humiliation is only the reflection of what happens to God's Equal in his self-emptying. The death on the cross is indeed only the unfolding of the incarnation. There, on Golgotha, the meaning of the incarnation, the meaning of Bethlehem, breaks through and comes into view. And this—he who humbles himself even to death on the cross, he who doubly (i.e. also in his humanity) obscures himself—this is the heavenly Head of his Church! And should it then be possible that anyone in that Church seeks his own, does not set the other above himself and so mind the 'one thing'?

And now the argument takes a new turn, which certainly does not at all mean a turn to something different, but serves more than ever to concentrate attention on the one compelling point that has now been attained: **Therefore God has exalted him and given him the name above all names.** Why does Paul add this and all that follows? Only for the sake of dogmatic completeness, or in order to secure a comforting, triumphant end to the story of Christ descending into the depths? One might think that the real purpose in pointing to Christ had been fully worked out in what has already been said. So in fact it *has*. But what is now *added* underlines emphatically and surely not superfluously: *this* is the Lord and Head of the Church, *there* is where we stand *en Christō Iēsou* (in Christ Jesus), *therefore* God exalted him, it is *as such*—as the One who emptied and humbled himself—that Christ stands where we see him stand, in glory at the right hand of God. There is good reason for what the ancient painters did when in their representations of Christ ascending to heaven and throned in heaven they left the wounds from the cross. That is the meaning of the *dio* (therefore). It does not say that he who was humbled and humiliated was afterwards exalted, was indeed (a much disputed point in discussions of this passage at the time of the Reformation) rewarded for his self-denial and obedience. But what it says is, that precisely he who was abased and humbled even to the obedience of death on the cross is also the Exalted Lord. Notice that there is no mention of any reassumption of the 'form of God'. No, he who became Man and was crucified, whose abasement and humiliation is not by any means washed out or cancelled—it is *he* who is exalted, it is to *him* the great name is given, it is of *him*, as the Equal of God that he never ceased to be, but as the Equal of God who abased and humbled himself, that all that follows is said. There is no other Christ than this, God's Equal become Man.

Notice further that it is said most emphatically: therefore *God* exalted him. In the case of the abasement and humiliation it was 'himself', and we had there to point out how this *heauton* (himself) bars the door to all attempts to penetrate and comprehend the divinity of the Man Jesus directly on our own account: in his personal, innermost being he has assumed the form of a servant. The sequel, 'God has exalted him', cannot of course serve to introduce another, second subject of will and action; but the very change of person now impresses on us again, this time from the positive side, that the door which was here barred by God's Equal, the Son, can also be opened again solely by 'the God', the Father. Once again: flesh and blood *cannot* reveal *that*. To take the picture of his abasement and humiliation, of his death on the cross, and discover in it among other things also something that from the human point of view is directly evident and compelling, and then to find in *that* (say, in the ethos of his obedience) his *exaltation*, to see *in that* his *Lordship*—*that* is not the way to understand Jesus as Lord. No, the emptying and humbling must take its course to the bitter end, *mechri thanatou* (to death), the door must be bolted, till in fact *nothing* remains but the word God alone can speak—the word *resurrection*. Only when it is *not* infringed does this picture remain what, as a manifestation of saving grace, it certainly *also* is: a *law* that claims and sanctifies. It is a law because (in our context it is doubtless *for that very reason* that reference is made to the fact) God *acknowledges* him in his abasement and humiliation, because Jesus is *risen* from the dead, because in the servant form he *is* God's Equal. There can be no getting round this exclusive, paradoxical meaning of the *hyperhypsōsen* ([God]) has exalted [him]). Only the resurrection makes knowledge possible here. God must here be at the same time both light and eye, both the goal and the way to it. He *is* that, says Paul. *He* has given Jesus the name above all names, did not suffer him in the form of a servant to depend on grace in vain. The 'name above all names' is, according to v. 11, the name *Kyrios*. That is a different thing from the 'form of God' of v. 6, something that takes the place of it and might very well be called the *new* God-form of the Revealer and Reconciler. God the *Lord* is the God who calls his own, gathers, illumines, justifies, purifies and prepares them for his kingdom. This name now belongs (that is the power of his resurrection) to the abased and humbled One.

God has exalted him to be the Lord, in him he has established himself as Lord of the kingdom of grace on earth, **that in the name of Jesus every knee should bow, of heavenly beings and earthly beings and those under the earth, and every tongue confess: Jesus Christ is the Lord to the glory of God the Father.** The purpose of God's grace in giving Jesus the name 'Lord' is, that through him his people may be gathered, his Church constituted, that in *this name*, in *this* Lord, under *his* law, within *his* order, God may be worshipped by every creature which, having been created in God's image, can worship God, needs reconciliation with God and is capable of it. God's Equal has found his right in this—that *in* his abasement and humiliation he is *Lord* over all. God has found his glory in this, that he prepares his kingdom in incomprehensible condescension. And that is the right and the glory that now count also for those who are his, for his Church—the right and the glory of *tapeinophrosynē* (humility), manifestly identical with the law, the law of grace (v. 2), that bids us 'mind the one thing'.

12-13. Two points should first be noticed regarding the construction. Firstly, the principal verb of the whole complex is *katergazesthe*; on it depends also the *kathōs* clause, which should be put between brackets or dashes; and to this *kathōs* clause, but still dependent on *katergazesthe*, belongs also the elliptical clause beginning *mē hōs*. Secondly, to understand the verses in themselves and in their context, the following words should be underlined: *hōste . . . meta phobou kai tromou . . . theos gar estin . . . kai to . . . kai to. . . .*

The curtain in front of the picture shown in vv. 6-11 has first of all dropped again. After the great reminder of the Reality of Christ, in which the apostle's conversation with the congregation takes place, we again find ourselves in the middle of the conversation itself. What purpose was the reminder meant to serve? It was meant, as we saw in the discussion of v. 5, to make the imperative that dominates vv. 1-5 ('mind the one thing'), the exhortation to humility among themselves, so to speak into an *indicative*. It was meant to set the apostolic *paraklēsis* (admonition) of v. 1 in the light of its origin, in which light it is distinguished from any kind of mere moral instruction by the weight, the necessity, the absoluteness, the sheer compelling urgency of the law of God fulfilled in Christ—a fulfilment in which Christians as such exist, so that anything other than fulfilment would necessarily mean for them the impossible, the return to nonexistence. The reminder of the concrete meaning of *en Christō Iēsou* (in Christ Jesus), of the *kenōsis* (emptying) and *tapeinophrosynē* (humility) in which Jesus Christ is exalted by God to be Head of his Church, is the *foundation* for Paul's seemingly groundless demand, its authentication to the conscience of the Christians as such, who through grace (be it well understood—through grace!) *are* bound to obey it.

Therefore, my beloved, Paul now begins again. Now that the words of vv. 6-11 have been spoken, he knows himself more completely in agreement with his readers as to the fact that what he wants of them is really *relevant* to them and is a thing *they* too *must* want. He uses a similar formula, e.g. in I Cor. 15.58 to make the transition from doctrine back to life, which certainly does not at all mean a *metabasis eis allo genos* (a digression to something different in kind). If indeed they wanted anything else, then it must be that they *were* not really *en Christō Iēsou* (in Christ Jesus) at all, as was supposed in v. 5, that they really did not *recognize* the name Kyrios given to Jesus by God. Paul has not the slightest intention of considering that even for a moment. The *hōste agapētoi mou*, 'therefore, my beloved', by its very silence on the point, decisively dismisses the possibility. He is in a position to draw consequences and conclusions from their *en Christō Iēsou einai* (their being in Christ), or rather once again to *underline*, to maintain now simply as an essential part of their own real existence, what he had put to them earlier in vv. 1-5 as a demand.

With the *kathōs* clause, which belongs in parenthesis, he adds first of all: **As indeed you were always obedient.** The obedience in question is, looking back to vv. 1 ff. in the first instance undoubtedly to be explained as obedience towards Paul. The authority with which Paul commands them *axiōs politeuesthe* 1.27, *touto phroneite* 2.5 (your state must be *worthy* of the Gospel;

mind *that*), and now *meta phobou kai tromou katergazesthe* (work out *with fear and trembling*)—that authority is not new to them, nor do they regard it with reluctance, for indeed they have long known its ground in the Reality that *makes* it authority. He can recognize and remind them that, living with him in that same Reality, they have obeyed his word before and that it is a question of *remaining* on the path which is their own most proper path in life.

Not as something that must happen **only in my presence, but now much more in my absence.** Intrinsically this elliptical clause of course forms a further explication of the foregoing reference to continued obedience to his instructions. Nevertheless it would accord better with Paul's style—with the way his thought keeps racing ahead—if the missing verb were sought in the imperative *katergazesthe* (work out) that dominates the whole sentence. Paul wishes the foregoing reminder of the obedience they have so far maintained towards him, and therewith also the specific demand he is now making on them, to be guarded against a misunderstanding that is perhaps not entirely ruled out—as if what they have to do would or could depend on the immediate impression made by his own personality, as if the authentication of his demand at the bar of their conscience would or could consist in their being mentally caught off their guard and swayed by his appearing and speaking to them in person, by the natural and spiritual influence of the man Paul as such. The appeal to their *en Christō Iēsou einai* (their being in Christ Jesus) and therewith to his apostolic authority has nothing to do with direct influence of that sort. The demand is thoroughly valid even without regard to his own person and its influence—indeed, it is precisely without regard to them that it is valid. Paul wishes to see his apostolic authority distinguished from the personal authority which he is well aware of possessing. That is why he does not write, 'but also in my absence', but, 'now much more in my absence'. When Paul uses the word *nyn* (now) it must always be taken into account that he means a very much qualified 'now'—a *nunc aeternitatis* (a now with the character of eternity) can come very near it. And likewise the expression *pollō mallon* (much more) in Paul's usage means as a rule that he wishes to make a distinction of so to speak catastrophic proportions (cf. especially the use he repeatedly makes of the expression in Rom. 5). He wishes to say: now of all times, now that I am absent, you stand in *God's* presence and not in mine. Not only are the presence and absence of the person declaring the law of no consequence for its validity, but it is more especially in the absence of the human person declaring it that the law has to be respected as *law*, i.e. as instituted in the presence of the God who is the real and primary Giver of it.

And now the decisive and most emphatic words of the whole complex: **with fear and trembling** work out your salvation! That they are decisive and emphatic I conclude (*a*) from the fact that when they occur in Paul elsewhere, namely I Cor. 2.3; II Cor. 7.15; Eph. 6.5, they are likewise decisive and emphatic, (*b*) from the fact that they precede the main verb and its object, (*c*) from the fact that no reasonable meaning whatever that makes sense in the context of the passage can be gained from them unless the whole emphasis of the sentence is allowed to fall on them. But what then does 'with fear and trembling' mean? What Kierkegaard in his well-known work understood by it is another matter, that does not concern us here. What Paul understood by it can be plainly inferred from the two parallel passages named. In both the expression denotes *humility*, consciousness of one's own insignificance—and that not so much, at any rate not directly, in God's presence, but in relation to other men. In I Cor. 2.3 the expression is joined with *astheneia* (weakness): 'I determined not to know anything among you except Jesus Christ, and him as the Crucified. And I came to you in weakness and in much fear and trembling, and my word and my message did not consist of persuasive words of wisdom.' And in II Cor. 7.15 the Corinthians are commended because, when Titus had to represent Paul in a dispute among them, they had received him 'with fear and trembling'. In the same sense the expression stands finally also in Eph. 6.5: 'Servants, obey your masters after the flesh with fear and trembling!' In our passage also we must abide by the sense indicated by these parallels. It is purely and simply a case of the *tapeinophrosynē* (humility) of each before the others, which was demanded in v. 3 and was shown in vv. 6-11 to be what makes

Jesus the Head of the Church and therefore Christians Christians. In fear and trembling, i.e. in startled humility, in the consciousness of having nothing to assert in one's own favour and against the others, it must come about—the reminder of grace, of Christ Jesus as the place where by reason of their baptism Christians exist, is sufficient—that the demand authenticates itself to their conscience and the act of obedience that necessarily results from that is performed.

But of course what Paul says is: with fear and trembling **work out your salvation,** and the syntactical dependence of 'with fear and trembling' on these words makes it understandable enough that the point and accent of the sentence has almost always been sought in them. They have become a crux of Protestant dogmatics and a repeatedly quoted *dictum probans* of the Catholics, because they were thought to contain a solemn summons on Paul's part, which the addition of 'with fear and trembling' served to intensify: 'Man, see to your salvation! Do all you possibly can towards it!' The old dispute is now softened, however, when it is perceived that in the whole sentence nothing was further from Paul's mind than *that* command. It must be granted that man's activity in grace, in the appropriation of salvation, is here asserted—and very vigorous activity at that. Paul never conceived man *in actu conversionis* (in the act of conversion) as *lapis aut truncus* (as stock or stone), but—however much or little that may mean—certainly as man, and that is, as man in action, as *katergazomenos* (working). But let us now ask ourselves in what sense it could have occurred to Paul in the present context to summon to such action, how isolated the command would be, at all events from what has gone before—quite apart from the fact that the expression 'with fear and trembling' must thereby have a meaning given to it which, in the parallels at all events, it does not bear. From the dogmatic point of view the passage is of no account—that is obvious as soon as we allow the 'with fear and trembling' its natural emphasis and consequently grant that the 'work out your salvation' here bears *no* emphasis and does not stand on its own account. It is a shortened expression for: to *live* as a Christian, to *show* and *prove* oneself what one is as a Christian. The salvation, the promised final

deliverance which the Christian as such awaits, claims the movement, the activity, the work, the life of the whole man. The truth
of that is presupposed here as self-evident, and it is not until vv. 15
and 16 that the accent and emphasis will fall on it. Here, however,
in v. 12 Paul wishes to say *how* it is to be done and what it all more
especially depends on. He has the situation of vv. 1–5 in view: the
Philippians who would certainly like to work out their salvation,
who would certainly like to be Christians, but thereby get in
their own way with their assertiveness and vanity and their each
considering his own point of view. He wishes to tell them what
it takes: fear and trembling is what it takes! In the reality of the
Kingdom of Christ, everyone who there puts his future salvation
into practice is placed in a position of humility. He is put there by
remembering the grace in which he participates in Jesus Christ.
Anyone who refused to let himself be put there, would not be in
Christ Jesus, would by his very refusal betray the fact that his life
has as yet nothing to do with the future salvation.

And now we must also be able to understand v. 13: **For it is
God who accomplishes in you both the willing and the
accomplishing according to his good pleasure.** Here Augus-
tinian and Protestant dogmatics would seem to be one up with
its doctrine of the sole efficacy of divine grace. But here too cau-
tion is the order of the day. Here too the very thing that is not
emphasized is the one that is usually seized on at once—the relation of God and man and the absoluteness of the divine activity
and human passivity respectively. But again the accent falls on the
initial *theos estin ho energōn* (it is *God* who accomplishes in you),
and it is not in the first instance a case of the humbling of man
before God but of the humbling of the one before the other—
because it is *God* who gives each one whatever he accomplishes
in 'working out his salvation', who indeed gives him the very will
to it, because he is the real Accomplisher of all real salvation. The
reason why we should be Christians in fear and trembling and
not otherwise is, that as such we put ourselves entirely into the
power of God, that as such we recognize that all grace, that everything—the willing and the accomplishing, the beginning and the
end, the faith and the revelation, the questions and the answers, the

seeking and the finding—comes from God and is reality only in God. Everything here that *really* happens at all, has God as its Subject. Even the action of our own lives, through being claimed in grace for God, becomes an act in which God the Holy Spirit is himself the Subject, and glorifies himself. Man cannot put his salvation into practice except as he recognizes: it is *God*. . .! If we are fully to understand here, then we must look back to v. 9, where it was said in exactly the same tone: *dio kai ho theos auton hyperhypsōsen* (therefore God has exalted him). *God* gave Jesus the Kyrios-name. That now becomes relevant. What corresponds to the Kyrios-name in the Christians' case is the act of really and seriously putting into practice their future salvation. Both come from God, *hyper tēs eudokias* (according to his good pleasure). It is according to the good pleasure of God, in his freedom, that Jesus is the Lord, that we are Christians—in a word, that grace is reality. It is on the free will of God that everything depends, that the whole thing every moment depends—*therefore* (we now understand the mysterious *gar*, 'for', at the beginning of the sentence) one can face the other only in fear and trembling, in humility, without cause, courage or desire for *self*-assurance, *self*-assertion, *self*-justification.

In this way vv. 12 and 13 are linked together—but also only in this way. If they are given a different accent and interpretation, as is suggested, e.g. by Luther's translation, then the two verses stand side by side, not as a paradox but quite simply as a meaningless contradiction, from which only the most dubious artifices can wrest a meaning—quite apart from the fact that it will then never be understood what they are supposed to be doing or trying to do in this particular context, and quite apart from the fact that then there can be no foreseeable end to the dispute between Pelagians and Augustinians, Catholics and Protestants, because then the former can seize on v. 12 and explain v. 13 in its light while the latter with relatively equal right can do the same thing the other way round. The meaning and coherence of the two verses are assured (and as far as the dispute is concerned, a higher interpretation of the passage is gained *above* whatever has then still to be asserted on either side), when we resolve to assume that

after the great Christological excursus of vv. 6-11 Paul has not
entirely forgotten what he was speaking of in vv. 1-5, that the
hōste (therefore) at the beginning of v. 12 must have a recognizable relation to what went before it, and that the interpretation of
the expression 'with fear and trembling' cannot be freely invented
but must be governed by the Pauline parallels. In that case there is
then no more to be said: the passage is concerned purely and
simply with the humility in which alone men can meet each
other under grace, for Christ's and God's sake.

Do everything without grumbling and cavilling Paul
continues in v. 14. We must not be put off by the fact that the
whole pathos of the Pauline ethic is concentrated once again on
this apparently very special point. Again we do not know in
detail the circumstances here referred to. *Gongysmos* is grumbling,
murmuring, muttering, *dialogismoi* are cavils, scruples, niceties,
such as in fact arise inevitably in grosser or subtler form from a
Christian's failure to be humble, even when he is a Christian who
really does seek to put his hope into practice—things like the
eritheia (assertiveness) and *kenodoxia* (conceit) mentioned in v. 3.
Paul takes these things so seriously—so little as questions of more
or less perfect morality, and so much as the scene of the decisive
Christian 'Either-Or'—that it is on their account that he becomes
so urgent as in v. 1, and issues such ultimate reminders as in vv.
6-11. It is on their account that he speaks in v. 12 of 'fear and
trembling' and in v. 13 of God as the One whom the Christian
knows to be the sole Subject of his life's activity as such.

That too—we cannot escape the utter concreteness in which
Paul speaks—is obviously what he now has in mind also in the
following verses (15 and 16), where he offers a description of
what Christians are and in what capacity they are to exist in the
world, distinguished by grace from those who are not Christians.
Now it is this side of the matter that becomes the important one:
not the manner of their activity, but the nature of it, which before
he had no more than mentioned with the words 'work out your
salvation'. But what was said in the previous verses on the question of manner forms the background to what now follows—and
a background that must not be left out of account.

That you may be blameless and pure, spotless children of God in the midst of a crooked generation. The first words of v. 15 remind us at once of 1.10, where the Christian community was described in quite a similar way as something faultless, clean, irreproachable. But neither there nor here may we think of moral rectitude in our sense. The impure and faulty things of which Paul is speaking are *eritheia, kenodoxia, gongysmoi, dialogismoi* (assertiveness, vanity, grumbling, cavilling), all the things that come of not being humble, of not being broken, of not fearing and trembling, or rather all these 'nots' themselves. That must all be dropped. We rightly understand Paul if we are taken aback by the negativeness of this basic ethical demand from which all the further demands he appears to make can be derived. The Pauline demand is critical, not positive: for God's sake and Christ's sake away with all conscious personal eminence! *Down!*—that is the meaning of 'up' in Christ. There is pure air here, the sharp air of grace that takes away the element of personal claim and possession on man's part which in all working out of salvation, in all Christianity, constantly tends to arise, as if Christianity and Christian living consisted in anything other than in man's being cast in all his poverty upon God, that in God he may now be rich.

The next words in v. 15—*tekna theou amōma meson geneas skolias kai diestrammenēs* (spotless children of God in the midst of a perverse and crooked generation)—come from the LXX of Deut. 32.5 but are something in the nature of a triumphant parody of that passage, where the Israelites are called on the contrary stained children, a perverse and crooked generation. In contrast to that Paul calls the Christians children *of God*, and it is not *they* who are the perverse and crooked generation, the land and people of darkness, but as men who are spotless, i.e. who do not participate in the general disgrace and non-humility, they are to be something different in the midst of such a generation. It is not the pharisaic ideal of being better than the wicked world, that Paul is proclaiming here. We need only keep always in view the fact that what distinguishes the Christians from the others is really nothing positive: it is in *fear and trembling* that they are something different from other men, in fundamental renunciation of the wish to be

superior to other men. It is in humility that they journey towards
their salvation. It is in the struggle against themselves that they
fight the struggle for existence. Pharisaism is nothing new in the
world, no light in the darkness. That appears where men can no
longer join in the game of self-esteem, where man as such is
assailed and called in question.

Christians are such men. That is why it can be said of them:
**you shine among them like the stars in space, since you have
the Word of Life.** These words must not be turned into an
imperative—that is forbidden especially by their conclusion. We
have here a simple statement of fact: they possess, know, hear the
Word of Life. We think of vv. 6-11. Whoever has this Logos
(this Word), has life, i.e. deliverance from death. To seek one's
own in the sense of v. 4 means to fall a prey to *phthora* (decay).
Christ, who does not seek his own, is Life. And whoever belongs
to him cannot but shine in the world—and that, too, without
attempting anything special or displaying any special qualities.
The apologists of the second century were certainly no longer
moving on the original lines when they began to point the
heathen commendingly to the moral virtues of the Christians. As
bearers of the Word of Life they ought indeed to shine, but the
Word of Life is death to the poisonous germ of *all* self-glorification. That death is the shining light that becomes visible in them,
the reflection of the light of Christ, in which they resemble the
stars of the universe which illumine the night because they are
themselves illumined by the light of day. By their complete lack
of self-glorification, by living by grace in fear and trembling, they
represent without any special intention of doing so the order of
God amid the disorders into which the unhumbled man daily falls
and must fall—they are the breakwaters in the flood not by their
Christian activity, propaganda, agitation and mission, but by
their Christian existence.

Thus sanctified, Paul concludes, you exist, must exist, will exist
to my glory against the day of Christ. Such children of God
among a perverse generation are what Paul would like to bring
to his Lord as spoil—a 'joy and crown' also for him, the apostle
himself, as he will put it in 4.1, because in this way, and only in

this way, they will bear him witness that **he has not run in vain and laboured in vain.** He would not wish to have been at work in vain. But it is of course for Christ that he has been at work, and only the day of Christ can reveal the truth of the 'not in vain'. What else can it then mean for him but—with the success of having won men to the humility of Christ and held them fast in it. That is the light he would wish to have kindled. That will be his glory—until that day by its very nature a hidden, secret, invisible glory, but at that day unfailingly glorious.

REJOICE IN THE LORD!

But even if my blood is shed in the offering and consecration of
your faith—I joy and rejoice with you all. Even so you ought
also to joy and rejoice with me.—But I hope in the Lord Jesus
soon to be able to send Timothy to you, so that I may be encouraged by news of you. For I have no close associate who would
genuinely care for you; they are all concerned for their own
cause, not that of Christ Jesus. You know his record, that as
child to father he has served the Gospel with me. Him, then, I
hope to send as soon as I see my situation a little more clearly.
But I trust in the Lord that soon I myself shall be able to come
too.—I thought it urgent, however, to send you Epaphroditus,
my brother and fellow-worker and fellow-soldier, your envoy
to minister to my needs. For he was longing for you all and got
worried because you had heard of his illness. And he was indeed
mortally ill. But God had mercy on him—and not only on him
but also on me, lest I should have to have one grief on top of
another. So I am now sending him with all speed, so that you
too may be able to rejoice in seeing him and I may be free of
grief. Receive him in the Lord, then, with all joy, and hold such
men as him in high honour. For in the cause of the work of
Christ he came near death, risking his life in order to be your
representative in ministering to me. Finally, my brothers,
rejoice in the Lord!

Here we have a paragraph that does not contain any direct
'teaching'. Paul discusses a few points of a purely personal human
kind concerning the relationship and intercourse between himself
and the Philippian congregation. If we did not know the context,
it would be tempting to say that as far as the passage in itself is
concerned, it is not absolutely necessary to conclude that the
relationship and intercourse in question have any particular connexion with the cause of Jesus Christ. The cause of Jesus Christ,

apart from v. 17 and the frequently recurring *en kyriō* (in the Lord), goes incognito so to speak in these verses. The bond between writer and addressees could, from these verses, also be something else—e.g. a political association or some other spiritual movement, or perhaps even a great commercial enterprise whose leader we here see corresponding with his distant partners or representatives. Save that the extraordinary feeling and intimacy, flexibility and refinement of the manner in which it is done would certainly make us doubt that assumption again at once, and must call our attention to the fact that here at all events we have to do with a very striking kind of humanity. These passages in which we have seemingly nothing but just this peculiarly exalted humanity reflected in the discussion of long-forgotten matters of a concrete earthly kind—such passages, particularly in Paul, must not be simply disregarded. If they tell us nothing new about his purpose and his message, they show us so much the better what he did and how he actually lived. They are like parts of a picture book, illustrating first and foremost his ethical instructions: this is how he himself seeks to realize the things he has laid down for his congregations as the will of the Lord. But they illustrate also his theological thoughts: this is how it looks when a man does not only think these thoughts but, because they are true and necessary thoughts, must live constantly in their shadow and can never get away from them in his concrete decisions. In the case of the Epistle to the Philippians very special attention must also be given to the fact that outwardly it hangs more than others on the thread of a purely human relationship. Paul gives those who are anxious about him as soothing an account of his situation as possible, he encourages them in the difficulties which they on their part have to face, he commends to them the intermediaries who are bearers of the communications between him and them, he thanks them for the material support he has received from them. It does not particularly require a Paul for all that, but it now so happens that he *is* Paul in all that—this time indeed it is precisely on that that the stress falls, and it is only in the form of digressions or lengthy interjections that we here find the pieces of real teaching in the narrower sense which have made the letter important and unforgettable for the Church and no doubt already for the first readers.

A peculiar difficulty attaching to just such passages as the present one must, however, also be mentioned here right at the start. Picturing the concrete circumstances in which we find the apostle speaking here is for us, if we refuse ourselves the liberty of expanding the written text in the manner of the story-teller (a liberty which few commentators really do *not* take to themselves!), unfortunately of little help. In what he says of Timothy, and more especially of Epaphroditus, Paul presupposes a great many things which the first readers either knew or could learn by word of mouth or were meant to read (and in a position to read) between the lines, but in regard to which we are thrown back entirely on conjecture. We must simply reconcile ourselves to that, even if it means that in many respects the attitude of Paul himself is shrouded for us in a certain obscurity. We should so much like to know e.g. all about Epaphroditus' life in Rome *apart* from the light Paul sheds on it for us, so as to be the better able to appreciate that light. In vain. In point of fact we have Epaphroditus solely in that light, which obviously (that much cannot be denied) is very favourable to him, and unless we wish to lose the solid ground of the text under our feet we have to abide by that, even though the text does not then tell us all we should certainly like to know.

In explanation of our paragraph it must first of all be noticed that it would not be impossible after 1.26 to pass over the whole of 1.27-2.16 and without missing anything to continue reading here at 2.17. The *alla* (but) with which v. 17 begins can certainly also be set in relation to v. 16—Paul interrupts the exhortation to humility, which he had had in view from 1.27 on and which reached its climax in 2.12 f., and now declares with a confidence that seems almost brusque: I rejoice, rejoice with you all! 'He who has begun the good work in you will also complete it!' will have to be added from 1.6. An immediate relation of that sort certainly does exist, but considering the main content of v. 17, which surely really lies in the parenthetical clause with *ei kai* (even if), it cannot well be supposed that that exhausts the relation of the *alla* (but) to what has gone before. **Even if my blood is**

shed in the offering and consecration of your faith—that has
obviously no relation to all that directly or indirectly preceded it,
to the whole exhortation of 1.27-2.16. Perhaps it could be connected with 1.30 (but certainly only by disregarding the context
of that verse). Its best and surest link is obviously with 1.24-26
where (following our interpretation of that passage) Paul at the
climax of his deliberations concerning life and death in vv. 21 ff.
had declared that he saw himself under a constraint that put an
end to all deliberations and made it necessary for him to remain in
the flesh for your sakes (*di' hymas*) as the apostle of his congregations. He had gone on to say that, counting on that, he knew of
no other possibility than that he should remain with them to their
increase and joy in the faith and that he should increase their
'glory in Christ' by a new visit to Philippi. At this point the
admonitory digression of 1.27-2.16 set in with a wide sweep. At
exactly this point also, now that the digression is over—so the
alla (but) has certainly also to be taken as the closing bracket of a
parenthesis that reaches a long way back—comes the continuation
and addition: if, however, everything should turn out very
differently from what is supposed in 1.24-26, if Paul instead of
living to the increase and joy of their faith should *die*, shed his
blood (literally, be himself poured out as a libation) in the consecration and offering of their faith—then I rejoice that way too,
that way too with you *all*. Thus the concept *pistis hymōn* ([offering
and consecration of] your faith) also forms a bracket that joins
2.17 to 1.24. Paul here regards the faith of the Philippians, and
implicitly of course the faith of his congregations in general, as an
act of offering and consecration such as his readers constantly had
before them in pagan religious services. The same idea underlies
Paul's comparing himself in Rom. 15.16 with the priest who
officiates at such sacrifices. Here it is with the drink offering there
sacrificed—this of course in view of his possibly approaching
execution. The ceremonial form in which Paul introduces this
tragic 'if' shows at once that he wishes to divest it of all tragedy in
the eyes of his readers, to put them so to speak on familiar terms
with it as perhaps a necessary practical consequence of his relation
to them and their faith. We recall from 1.7, 16, 20 how for him

apostleship, grace, giving public account of himself, and now perhaps a further spell of life, perhaps indeed a martyr's death, formed one single whole. The crown of the whole can be either the one or the other. It was therefore not without reserve that Paul in 1.25-26 gave the comforting assurance without in any way wishing simply to put the second possibility out of their minds. Apostleship could also mean death—that way too it would be service to their faith, and that way too they would consequently require to assent to it.

And so. Even if (contrary to the expectation of 1.25-26) *that* should now be what it means, **I joy and rejoice with you all. Even so you ought also to joy and rejoice with me!** The connexion of the 'I rejoice' and 'you ought also to rejoice' with the immediately preceding verse is, as we have said, not to be denied. It naturally marks also the jubilation in which Paul breaks off his admonition in the awareness that those he is speaking to really will be his glory at the day of Christ, that he will not have run and laboured in vain for their sakes (v. 16). Have done with all imperatives! Let us rejoice—I with you and you with me! If we think back to vv. 5-11 and what was there shown to be the background of the admonitory digression, then the change here, the sudden breaking off, will not unduly surprise us. But beyond that the *chairō* (I rejoice) and *chairete* (rejoice!) are obviously, and much more, the trumpet call with which Paul sets an end to the anxiety in which the Philippians think of him and to his own attempts to comfort them by holding out hopeful prospects. I would have you know that even in face of the worst possibility I rejoice—and indeed I rejoice with you, with all of you. Why? Because then, even then, even if in rather a different way, the same thing happens as was promised in 1.25-26 in the case of the first possibility—for the benefit of you all and in the service of your faith, the thing that to God's glory must happen on earth in accordance with the Lordship of Jesus Christ in heaven. I am what I am—and so if now no longer the sacrificing priest then the poured-out libation, but either way nothing else. Should I not rejoice in that—and indeed rejoice with you, who are certainly as much concerned as myself in what I am? And—inescapable consequence—should you not also of necessity rejoice with me, when everything one way or the other takes the course it must take in the service of the faith which I proclaimed to you and which is your own faith—when in the whole complex of apostleship and grace, which is what gives meaning also to our personal relationship, there can never be any gap but, one way or the other, only greater glory? This paradoxical *chairō* (I rejoice) and *chairete* (rejoice!), which met us already in 1.18, which forms the beginning as also the end of the present paragraph, and which then returns with emphatic repetition in 4.4, may well be termed the very heart and hub of our epistle. There exists a point above—absolutely above—all earthly problems, and at that point is joy. Yet what Paul says is not that, but in verbal form: 'I rejoice!', 'do you rejoice!'. It is only in action that this superior point is to be attained. It is as one engaged in such action that Paul confronts his readers; to drag them so to speak into the same action is his purpose for them. In no other letter is that expressed with such warmth and urgency as here—and here just by reason of the peculiarly personal human relationship between him and his readers.

To understand what follows, it must be remembered that 1.26 threw up the question when and how the Philippians were to hear more of Paul, or perhaps see him again in person. The first answer to that is the announcement of Timothy in vv. 19-24. **But I hope in the Lord Jesus soon to be able to send Timothy to you.** It will be well, here and in what follows, not to disregard the phrase *en kyriō Iēsou* (in the Lord Jesus) or *en kyriō* (in the Lord) as if it were a sort of figure of speech. We know already from 2.5 how important it is—that it is in fact the fundamental designation of the sphere, the union, the bond within which everything has here to be said, the purpose and the norm, the confidence and the reserve with which it has all to be said. If after the deadly serious words of v. 17 Paul is here already hopeful again—and hopeful too, according to v. 23, of a happy outcome to his trial—then we can see from that how in actual fact he was prepared with equal confidence for life and death. Between v. 17 and v. 19 there is a relationship entirely similar to that between 1.21 and 1.26.

Timothy, according to 1.1, was joint author of the letter; that he is spoken of here and in the following verses only in the third person gave us reason to suppose in 1.1 that the inclusion of the younger man there was a significant literary custom and no more. And now the ground for sending Timothy: **so that I may be encouraged** (strengthened) **by news of you.** Paul could have written: to see that all is in order among you, as his envoys were in fact wont to do, and as was doubtless not at all superfluous even in Philippi. He turns it round the other way and says: in order to bring me good news of you and thereby give me courage. Or the meaning may be: it is not by any means merely a case of Timothy's encouraging the Philippians with good news about Paul, but every bit as much the other way round. Paul needs them as they need him. The words perhaps combine a subtle, unobtrusive admonition and an expression of affectionate solidarity between apostle and congregation.

For I have no close associate who would genuinely care for you: they are all concerned for their own cause, not that of Christ Jesus. I should like to explain these two verses along with Hofmann as follows: *Tacheōs* (soon) he will send Timothy, it was said in v. 19—which however means: not just yet. V. 23 then supplies the reason for the 'not yet'. Timothy is thus excluded from vv. 20-21. In these verses Paul says why he does not at the moment send anyone else either. For the reason that he has no one else. He does have *isopsychoi*, sympathizers, adherents, associates (that must be the meaning of *isopsychoi* according to the LXX of Ps. 55.13). But there is none among them to whom he would like to entrust the care of the Philippian congregation, for they are all concerned for their own cause, not that of Christ Jesus. *O quam multi sua causa pii sunt!* (O how many are pious only from self-interest!), is Bengel's paraphrase. Yet Paul does not say *multi* (many) but *omnes* (all). This judgment has been termed harsh and impatient. It has been said that at least those mentioned in Col. 4.11, 14 must have been tacitly excepted. Why so? The reproach made in v. 21 is really no other than what was also held against the well loved and highly commended Philippian congregation itself at the beginning of this chapter. The interpretation has been suggested that no one was willing to take on himself the sacrifice of the long journey to Macedonia—or (recalling the conditions mentioned in 1.17) that they were all toeing a party line too closely to be able to carry out such a commission to one of his congregations in the way the apostle meant it. All that is no more than conjecture. We have to abide by the fact that Paul at the moment does not trust any of the Christians around him to do in Philippi *gnēsiōs*, genuinely—wholly objectively, in the way that is necessary—what he wishes to see done there. From the similarity, frequently overlooked by expositors, between the expression *ta heautōn zētein* (they are concerned for their own cause) and *ta heautōn skopein* (each [not] considering his own point of view) in 2.4, it may perhaps be concluded that Paul felt the Christians around him suffered from the same evil as according to the beginning of chapter 2 also afflicted so many in Philippi—too much so for any of them to be fitted to bring the help Paul wished for them. So therefore the Philippians must wait till Timothy is free.

Regarding him Paul does not harbour this misgiving, and to him he now returns: **You know his record, that as child to father he has served the Gospel with me.** The word order shows that it is not his person that is to be emphasized but his record—which likewise speaks in favour of the above interpretation of vv. 20-21. *Teknon* (child) was Paul's description of Timothy also in I Cor. 4.17; I Tim. 1.18; II Tim. 2.1 Notice how the picture shifts under the pressure of fact. Paul meant at first to say: he has served me with the faithfulness of a child towards his father. But then he corrects himself and says: with me he has served the Gospel with childlike faithfulness—that is, without seeking his own in the sense of v. 21. That is his record, which is known to the Philippians, and which fits him for the intended mission to them. V. 23 now gives the ground for the delay in sending him. **Him, then, I hope to send as soon as I see my situation a little more clearly.** *Aphidein* is: to see something from a distance. He means the outcome, and that the happy outcome, of his trial in Rome. So long as that still hangs in the balance he cannot do without him—for what specific reasons, we do not know. Then he will come—and then of course as at once the bringer of good news.

And now still more: **But I trust in the Lord that soon I myself shall be able to come.** Calvin is no doubt right when he interprets the *en kyriō* (in the Lord) especially here by saying that this repetition of the promise of 1.25 is of course meant *quasi suspensa in arcano Dei consilio* (as to a certain extent dependent on the secret counsel of God). But that by no means alters the fact that in view of this verse, compared with 2.17, we cannot marvel enough at the compass in which Paul contrives to speak of his own life (in exact correlation to his theology!) always with the same absoluteness whether in fear or in hope.

That, then, in the first instance, is the answer to the Philippians' question about further news of Paul or a reunion with him: for the moment you must wait, soon I hope to send Timothy, soon I hope indeed to be among you again in person as well.

The second and longer part of our paragraph, vv. 25-3.1a, is concerned with a man we do not meet elsewhere in the New Testament—the Philippian *Epaphroditus*, who is at present in Rome and now returning as bearer of the letter. The man had been sent to Rome not only to bring the apostle a gift of money from the congregation for his personal needs, but evidently with the commission to be of assistance to him also in other ways (again we do not know in what way). Now, however, he was suffering from something like homesickness, in addition to which he had taken ill, had then certainly recovered again, but now plainly wanted to break off his mission and return to Philippi. We can hardly fail to recognize that Paul, who according to Acts 15.38 had once separated from his first partner Barnabas because of a similar deserter, could have spoken very differently of this one, if the remarkable 'joy' in which Paul now lived and wrote had not protected him from that. What is now said of him forms (without one word of blame or even of irony) a single golden bridge built for his retreat. Everything—really everything—is done in order that even in face of this rather upsetting event the 'rejoice!' with which the paragraph begins and ends should still be made possible for the Philippians—naturally to the advantage of Epaphroditus.

I (so Paul at once assumes himself the responsibility for what
has happened) **thought it urgent** (in contrast to the delay in the
departure of Timothy) **to send to you** (notice that the idea of
sending back is avoided) **Epaphroditus, my brother and
fellow-worker and fellow-soldier** (all of course carefully
chosen words—Paul, whom we hear passing such severe judgment in v. 21, will have had his reasons for acknowledging all
this of the man), **your envoy** (*apostolos* means deputy, as in II Cor.
8.23—the receivers of the Jewish temple tax also bore this title)
to minister to my needs (we shall see in 4.10 ff. how Paul accepted and acknowledged the material help of the Philippians in a
ritualistic context, hence the expression *leitourgos*—really =
'sacrificial priest' or 'minister of the sanctuary'). The reason is:
**For he was longing for you all and got worried because
you had heard of his illness. And he was indeed mortally
ill.** The best possible, kindest and most complimentary interpretation of a situation which it is plain could rightly and justly also
have been presented in a different light! Yet it is not now a question of right and justice, but of the man's coming to Philippi in
all his frailness as a messenger of joy, a living illustration of the
grace in which God accepts each man ultimately just as he is and
whatever his condition. That is how Paul sees him: that is how
the Philippians are also to see him in the somewhat questionable
circumstances in which he comes back among them. He longed
for you all—one might well ask with suspicious curiosity, was it
really not just for his own family? He was worried about your
worry for him—really? what a very strange motive for the behaviour of a grown man! But all that is simply no concern of
ours, and would be no concern of ours even if we had a great deal
more cause for suspicion. He *was* in actual fact mortally ill, Paul
adds in support of his justification. **But God had mercy on him
—and not only on him but also on me, lest I should have to
have one grief on top of another.** They are to receive him as
one on whom God has had mercy, and thereby as a proof of the
divine mercy also received in his person by Paul himself. Paul
could not take his part more strongly or more deeply than that.
That Paul speaks of his *lypē* (grief), from the increase of which by

the death of Epaphroditus God has preserved him, shows incidentally that his *chairō* (I rejoice) has nothing to do with stoic apathy, but is much rather a paradoxical *chairō*, a mastery of genuinely existing grief, not so much attained in defiance as bestowed by God's grace. That Paul had occasion for such grief can be seen from 1.15; 2.21. **So I am now sending him with all speed, so that you too may be able to rejoice in seeing him and I may be free from grief.** Once again Paul takes the matter upon *himself*: the return is not merely for the benefit of Epaphroditus, but his appearance among the Philippians is to give them joy, and Paul himself would like to be free of the grief that is caused him by the other's grief. **Receive him in the Lord, then, with all joy,** not with ill humour, not with all too facile reproaches, **and hold such men as him in high honour,** not because of their person, not because of their merits, not even because of their faithfulness, but because of their service: **in the cause of the work of Christ he came near death, risking his life in order to be your representative in ministering to me.** That is: you yourselves sent this man out to the *ergon Christou* (the work of Christ), by which is meant the assistance of the apostle. He made up for what had of necessity to be lacking in your assistance, namely your persons (cf. for this use of *hysterēma* I Cor. 16.17). His entry into the service of this cause brought him (Paul certainly means: not by chance) to the verge of the grave. From there he now comes back to you again. Receive him in that capacity! In that capacity hold him in high honour! All the rest of the story need not trouble you. I, Paul, take it upon myself. Yet Paul does not say he is taking anything upon himself. He simply does it. He commands: receive him in the Lord with all joy!

That is the second part of the answer: Paul, then, is not coming yet, Timothy not yet either, but here directly is the man from their own midst, their messenger, whom Paul now makes his. May they receive him in the spirit in which he sends him: *en kyriō meta pasēs charas* (in the Lord with all joy). With this thought Paul puts the first of the finishing touches to his letter: **Finally, my brothers, rejoice in the Lord!**

RIGHTEOUSNESS FROM GOD[1]

3.1b-4.1

To repeat myself in what I write to you is no burden to me, but a safeguard for you. Beware of dogs! Beware of wicked work-heroes! Beware of concision! For we are the circumcision, we who through the Spirit of God are religious, and glory in Jesus Christ, and do not rely on flesh—I have also things I could rely on where flesh is concerned. If anyone else thinks he can rely on flesh, then I could do so much more: circumcized on the eighth day, of the people of Israel, of the tribe of Benjamin, a Hebrew of Hebrew parents, as regards my attitude to the Law a Pharisee, as regards my zeal a persecutor of the Church, as regards my legal righteousness blameless. But what was gain to me I saw as loss for the sake of Christ. Now too, indeed, I see it all together as loss because of the victorious knowledge of Christ Jesus my Lord through whom that has all become loss to me, and I consider it dung, in order to gain Christ and be found in him—not with my righteousness from the Law, but with that which comes by faith, the righteousness from God on terms of faith—in order to know him and the power of his resurrection and the fellowship of his sufferings, to enter into the form of his death, in the hope that so I may be on the way to the resurrection of the dead. Not as if I had already apprehended or had already reached the goal, but I race on in the hope that I may apprehend, seeing that I am apprehended by Christ Jesus. Brothers, I con-sider myself not to have already apprehended. One thing, how-ever, is true: forgetting what is behind, stretching out to what lies ahead, I race towards the goal, towards the prize consisting in the calling in Christ Jesus which is valid above. We, then, who are perfect, let us think on that! And if you should think differently about anything, then God will give you revelation also in that. Only, let us continue in the direction in which we have come! Be followers of me, brothers, and watch those who walk according to the example you have seen in us. For many walk, whom I have often described to you—but now describe in

[1] *On the New Man's Way of Life* (O. Schmitz, *Aus der Welt eines Gefangenen*, pp. 33 f.) is perhaps not the best heading for this paragraph.

tears—as enemies of the Cross of Christ, their end is destruction, their God the belly and their glory in their shame, who set their minds on earthly things. For our citizenship is in heaven. From there we await also the Deliverer, the Lord Jesus Christ, who will change our body in its humiliation into the form of his body in its glory, by means of the power with which he can subdue everything to himself. Therefore, my brothers, my beloved for whom I long, my joy and crown, stand fast like that in the Lord, my beloved!

The half verse 3.1a, *to loipon, adelphoi mou, chairete en kyriō* (finally my brothers, rejoice in the Lord!), has entirely the character of a conclusion, and could very well be followed by 4.21 f. Instead, we find an unexpected new start in 3.2, to which v. 1b obviously also belongs; and with that the apostle embarks for the second time on a great digression.[1]

1b does not refer to the preceding 'rejoice!' which, although it is a repetition of 2.18, is surely not of a kind to occasion such a remark. *Ta auta graphein*, **to repeat himself,** is Paul's intention much rather in what follows—namely, in the warning and admonition that begins in v. 2. It was obviously only as an afterthought, when he had already begun the conclusion, that Paul decided to discuss this new theme, and v. 1b apparently forms the transition. If Paul calls what he now wishes to say a repetition of something written earlier, then the reference is not to an earlier passage in our epistle but to some letter, perhaps several letters from the apostle to the congregation, which are unknown to us but to judge by the contents of the present chapter must have formed a parallel to very well-known passages in Galatians, Romans and perhaps also Colossians. Whether Polycarp's testimony to the existence of several Epistles to the Philippians is a confirmation of the present passage, or has on the contrary been occasioned by it, need not concern us here.

[1] The question of the literary unity of our Epistle is one on which there could already be food for thought in face of the relation of 1.27-2.16 to its context. In view of this paragraph, too, it is perhaps not to be dismissed out of hand. We leave it at that.

It is no burden to me, but a safeguard for you to take up the theme in question once again, says Paul. The sentence shows: (*a*) that it is a question whose discussion could be a delicate matter because what was to be said was not certain of a good reception, and was now repetition at that; (*b*) that in regard to the readers' attitude to this question Paul is, to say the least, not entirely free of a touch of apprehensiveness; (*c*) that he himself is so full of the subject that he obviously could not *refrain* from speaking of it, not even out of special consideration for his readers. In spite of this preparation, necessary as it certainly is in the context of the epistle, the warning in question still comes with alarming abruptness.

It comes (v. 2) with the threefold Beware! watch! keep a sharp eye on!—whom? what? **Dogs, wicked work-heroes, concision!** Obviously an alarm, a summons to vigilance: a danger threatens the congregation from a very definite quarter characterized by these three terms of abuse. Is it also in view of definite happenings in the Philippian congregation that the alarm is raised? There was mention also in 1.28 of *antikeimenoi* (opponents) of the congregation, but to judge by the context it is there a question of persecutors, not as here of seducers. Yet it could also be that the warning here sounded is not occasioned by the present state of the Philippian congregation, but either by the memory of their earlier state, or by contemporary happenings in other congregations, or by events that were taking place before the apostle's own eyes in the place where he now was, or by a general review of his life's work and its major problem. However that may be, against *these* people he must now once more give warning. Whom does he mean? V. 2 itself as well as vv. 5 f. point us unequivocally in the direction of *Judaism*. But according to vv. 7 ff. it must be a case of Jewish *Christians*, representatives and propagators of a Judaized *Christianity*. With regard to the Jews in themselves as the open enemies of the Christian churches, the *blepete* (beware) would obviously have no point, but there would certainly be point in it in the case of *Christians* who were in the act of consciously or unconsciously transforming Christianity back into Judaism.

To understand the three terms of abuse in v. 2 let us begin with the third: *katatomē* (concision). That is of course a word-play on *peritomē* (*circum*cision). *Peritomē* as opposed to *akrobystia* (strictly, 'foreskin') is, as is well known, in Paul often simply a term for Jews *in general* as opposed to the Gentiles (e.g. Gal. 2.8; Rom. 4.12). But now it was of course just the question of circumcision (Gal. 5.2 ff.; I Cor. 7.18 f.) that was the shibboleth of *the* Christians who wanted Christianity anchored and established in Judaism through the closest possible connexion with the Israelitic rites. *Katatomē* means *con*cision, mutilation, destruction. *That* is what they are doing with their *circum*cision! To think of the splitting of the Christian congregations that resulted from this kind of propaganda, seems to me over-subtle. How Paul thinks of the result of the *katatomē* is shown by the clause in v. 19: *hōn to telos apōleia*, their end is *destruction*. In that light the other two terms can now be explained. Why of all things *kynes*, dogs? Barking, biting, voracity, laziness, lolling around have been urged by expositors as evil attributes of dogs and applied with greater or less success to the people thus maligned. But it is surely nearer to hand to reflect that the dog for the Jews belonged to the *unclean animals*. The Jewish Christians preached ceremonial cleanness. Like the lash of a whip comes Paul's term: dogs!—unclean, *precisely* in your cleanness! (as later: *katatomē, precisely* in your *peritomē*!). Now we can also understand the *kakoi ergatai*. I translate it with Bultmann[1]: 'work-heroes', who think to achieve great things by what they do. *Wicked, evil* men of action, says Paul, *precisely* in your call for action. 'There are busy people who would be better idle', comments Calvin. The verse is thus not without rhyme or reason. If the explanation given is correct, it cannot by any means be taken, however amazing Paul's heated outburst, as purposeless abuse.

In v. 3 the accent is as follows: **We are the circumcision, we who** *pneumati theou* **(through the Spirit of God) are religious,** practise religious worship, **and glory** *en Christō Iēsou* **(in Christ Jesus), and do not rely on flesh,** do not put our confidence in **flesh.** The accusations of v. 2 contained in negative form the programme of the propaganda afflicting the Christian Church: cleanness, industry, circumcision. V. 3 declares: the people of God that bore *that* mark simply does not exist any more. *We* are the

---

[1] Cf. R. Bultmann, *Der Stil der pailinischen Predigt*, p. 105.

one real people of God. *Ours* are in truth the prerogatives whose name and semblance alone are still with Israel. Paul does not say: we Christians. He gives a *factual* description of the *hēmeis* (we). Firstly: we who *through the Spirit of God* are religious. The addition *theou* (of God) shows that *pneuma* (Spirit) here is not to be taken as opposed to letter, ritual, works, etc. God *himself* makes us devout, his Spirit takes our part before his own throne. The anxious question as to the proper religion does not exist for us. Paul does not mean that the Christian as against the Jewish ritual is to be extolled as the divine, spiritual form, but what he most certainly does mean is, that in Christianity through the *pneuma theou* (the Spirit of God) the question just mentioned is a thing of the past. Further: we who glory *in Christ Jesus*. The question as to what gives occasion for *kauchēma* (glory) and *kauchasthai* (glorying) is the point at issue between Paul and his opponents. Do knowledge of the Law, and the corresponding ceremonial and moral righteousness, supply the occasion for it? Or does the 'glory' begin at the point where all that ceases, where man lays down his arms, where God *entirely* alone begins to speak, utters his *Word of grace* which man can do *no more* than believe? Paul has said of this *kauchasthai* both positively and negatively much that is paradoxical—if I am not mistaken, there are perhaps few of his concepts in which he is so personally involved as just this one. Here he says the one thing only: we glory *en Christō Iēsou* (in Christ Jesus)—at a point and in a context which, precisely by including us most intimately, at the same time forms for all of us the boundary against ourselves. By our baptism, which portrays our death, we have in fact been set in that context. This side of that boundary we have therefore nothing to glory in. Finally: we who *do not* rely *on flesh*. Flesh is the human creature of this aeon, existing in his own way far from his Lord, unredeemed, and as such also unredeemable. Does there exist in him, in his intentions, capabilities and achievements anything certain, reliable, trustworthy when it comes to the necessary ordering of our relationship with God? The opponent of v. 2 answers yes; Paul, in the name of the real people of God, the real *peritomē* (circumcision), answers no. Cf. Rom. 2.28: the real circumcision is not that which is *en tō phanerō* (outward in the flesh). Thus v. 3. forms a *delimitation*. It is meant to show that it is pointless, as a 'Christian', as *peritomē kardias en pneumati* (circumcision of the heart in the Spirit, Rom. 2.29), to come back on problems of a religious system which for the *hēmeis* (for us) simply no longer *exists*.

4. Visibly stimulated by a *secondary* thought, but not for that reason without a definite purpose, Paul sets off on the further development of his warning by way of simply taking himself as an example of how it is, what a man's condition is, when he has got beyond these problems—in other words, when he considers himself *no longer* religious except through the Spirit of God, *no longer* able to glory except in Christ Jesus, *no longer* able to rely on flesh. What follows in vv. 4-14 could of course also have been presented, as in Romans and Galatians, in the form of general, theoretical thesis and antithesis. It accords with the character of the rest of Philippians that here the decisive word is spoken in the first person singular. People should have hesitated all the same to make the foolish remark that he now comes to the description of his 'inner experience'. As if man were only outwardly *sarx* (flesh), as if he now found in his *inner* being some ground and occasion for *pepoithēsis* (confidence) and *kauchēma* (glory). As if what Paul in the following verses wishes to exemplify from his own case were not presented, in *this* very way still more drastically than in a more theoretical one, as *abrogation* of the subject designated by the first person singular, as immediate proximity not of Paul to Christ but irreversibly of Christ to Paul!

The secondary thought which leads him on to this track comes to light in v. 4a. It occurs to him after he has written v. 3 : **I have things I could rely on where flesh is concerned.** That means: it is not the have-not's jealousy that makes him speak as he did in v. 3. If it came to that, I could *also* find a few things to say of my cleanness, industry, circumcision. Thus—it is to sound like a challenge—**if anyone else thinks he can rely on flesh, then I could do so much more.** It is assuredly '*could*' that must be supplied to the *egō mallon* (I much more), not 'can'. Paul *can* of course *no longer* rely on things whose reliability is for him a thing of the past.

Likewise in II Cor. 11.18 he tells his opponents that he *could* glory as much as they—and then he *does* it in actual fact (two whole pages long in Nestle), only to end in 12.11 with the declaration *gegona aphrōn* (now I have become completely senseless [in my exposition]), but you have compelled me to blow the whole bubble up myself till it burst. I Cor. 9.1 ff. and 14.18 could also be compared here. So the immediately following verses 5-6 must be taken as spoken in parenthesis, and put forward not without a touch of self-mockery.

5. **Circumcised on the eighth day,** in other words, correctly as prescribed in Lev. 12.3. **Of the people of Israel,** so not, say, as a proselyte—who knows if there were not among the zealous Jewish Christians particularly zealous fresh-baked Jews over whom Paul could score a small triumph with his affirmation of his racial purity. **Of the tribe of Benjamin:** important not only because Paul as one of 'good' family knew it at all, but because the tribe of Benjamin together with Judah had alone held to the Davidic royal house under Rehoboam (1 Kings 12.21 ff.). **A Hebrew of Hebrew parents,** thus no Hellenist, as the foregoing had already implicitly said: not one of the mass of the ten tribes that were scattered and estranged from the homeland. And now it goes on in loftier vein.

6. **As regards my attitude to the Law a Pharisee,**[1] thus an expert, a devotee, a partisan of the strictest religious tradition. **As regards my zeal a persecutor of the Church.** A bold step, one might say, when Paul ventures to urge even *this*: in mistakenness, blindness and hatred towards the Christ who met me in the *ekklēsia* (church), in anti-Christianity such as is an inherent necessary consequence of zeal for that religious system, I could certainly teach anyone a few lessons. Or has any of them ever been *so* zealous? (That Paul is speaking of Jewish *Christians* must be kept in view in order to appreciate properly the piquancy of this particular remark.) Finally: **as regards my legal righteousness blameless.** In outlook and conduct, in regard to worship and morals, I got so far that human judgment found *nothing* left to take exception to in me. But—and now comes the great 'But'! that closes the bracket.

[1] The prominence and the mounting climax of the threefold *kata* ought not to be so obscured as it is in the translations of Lueken and Dibelius.

7. But what was gain to me I all at once saw as loss for the sake of Christ. I supply 'all at once' in consideration of the *alla men oun ge* with the present tense *hēgoumai* (now too, indeed, I see it [as loss]) in the following verse—hence not in order to emphasize the suddenness of the change, for that is *not* what Paul emphasizes. He does not wish to tell of how he came to be of different mind, but of *Christ*: in point of fact it did happen 'all at once' and in fact it happened by means of a change of mind wrought in him, but what he wants to say is what *Christ* meant for him (and *still* means, as the next verse will say) in regard to that religious standing of his. Notice now that he does not only say: but what was gain to me I later saw as indifferent, as unimportant—no: as *loss*. To repent—one surely turns here involuntarily to this concept—does not mean to be liberalized, to become indifferent to what we formerly were, to the former objects of our devotion and the former conduct of our lives, but—to be horrified by it all. Not realizing that it means *nothing*, but that it means evil. Spinoza does not become a Reformer, but Luther does. The Pharisee Gamaliel does not become an apostle, but the Pharisee Saul does. *Zēmian hēgēmai* means: I perceived *loss*, detriment, *damnum*, precisely in what was dearest and most precious to me (what even now, vv. 5-6, I can still, if need be, describe as dearest and most precious). The heights on which I stood are *abysmal*. The assurance in which I lived is *lostness*; the light I had *darkness*. It is not that nil takes the place of the plus, but the plus itself changes to a *minus*. Recognition not of some imperfection but precisely of the guiltiness, perversity and reprobateness of his glorious Phariseeism, irreproachable and upright as it was *en sarki* (in the flesh), recognition of the indictment not on his wickedness but on his *goodness*—that is what came upon him *dia ton Christon* (for the sake of Christ), that was the meaning which Christ's work had for his attitude to these things.

8a. Now too, indeed, I see it all together as loss. Paul would not have the content of the *hēgēmai* (saw) of v. 7 taken as a passing *impression*, but as a *state of affairs* that was once seen (that is what the *hēgēmai* refers to), is grounded in itself, and stands immutably before him: *hēgoumai* (I see).[1] How does he come to assert that? He says: a *hyperechon*, a decisive, superior, victorious factor has occupied the centre of the picture and holds the arms of the balance, once they have changed their places, conclusively in their *new* position. This *hyperechon* is the **victorious knowledge of Christ Jesus my Lord.** It might even have to be rendered outright: 'my Lord Christ Jesus as he makes himself known'. For the one thing which at all events is meant here is: my *hēgeisthai* (strictly, 'view') is grounded not in *me* but in the *Object* of my knowledge, **through whom that has all become loss to me.** Because Jesus Christ is the Reality, the Real Factor, the Agent,[2] in whom the lofty is humbled, the solid shattered, assurance dispelled, man in his self-made goodness exposed, Israelitic man in the splendour of his religious system declared guilty before God— because this Jesus Christ is *my Lord*, so that in effecting all this he is absolutely authoritative for me, and because he has given me to *know* that he is my Lord—*therefore* I consider the whole thing loss, *therefore* this *hēgeisthai* is no mere view (*Ansicht*) but an insight (*Einsicht*) with which the matter must rest. And now further:

8b–9a. I consider it—*panta* (v. 8a): all that I called my best, such as cleanness, industry, circumcision (v. 2), all the advantages listed in vv. 5–6—**dung, in order to gain Christ and be found in him.** That is how the accent must be placed in order to see that this sentence is not a repetition but a vigorous continuation. It forms also syntactically the key to all that follows, up to and including v. 11. *Skybala* can without hesitation well be translated ordure, filth, dung, excrement: it is a case of something which, once thrown away, is never touched again nor even looked at. It is settled, fundamentally and immutably, that there can be *no* going back to—be it well noted, not my wickedness but—my goodness. That goodness is over and done with and *abides* under judgment, must not have any form of lurking-place *alongside* of

---

[1] Notice the accumulation of particles, *alla men oun ge kai*, by which the present tense *hēgoumai* is powerfully underlined.

[2] *Die Wirklichkeit, der Wirkliche, der Wirkende.* The word-play can hardly be reproduced in English—unless perhaps by Actuality, Actual Subject, Actuator (*Translator*).

Christ. Why not? Because otherwise *he*, Christ, is not what I *gain*: he can only abide in me, only be my *gain*, when, just as v. 7 says, I have *no* other *kerdos* (no other gain). And because otherwise I shall not be *found* in him, am not in *him* (*en autō*), secure in *his* riches—therefore *I* must be *poor*, destitute. Paul calls this Christ, to know whom compels him to regard his best as *skybala* (dung), *kyriou mou*—not in casual rhetoric, but in this context of all places with objective necessity. Here the meaning of the fact that Jesus Christ is *my Lord* becomes clear and full-toned—also in contradistinction to the use mysticism makes of the same possessive pronoun. Paul, as the sequel shows, would claim the *right* of Christ as *his* right. That, intrinsically, is the aim of the *kerdēsō kai heurethō* (in order to gain Christ and be found in him). The right of *Christ*, however, puts Paul in the *wrong*. In order to *gain* Christ and be *found* in him, he must look on *his* right as dung, as *skybala*, i.e. *not* look on it any longer.

9b. Not with my righteousness, the righteousness from the Law (will I *gain* Christ and be *found* in him), **but with that which comes by faith in Christ, with the righteousness from God** (which one has) **on terms of faith.** In this participial clause, syntactically dependent on the *kerdēsō kai heurethō*, Paul tells in what that condition *consists* and how it *comes about*—the condition in which he holds all the good he could glory in to be *skybala* (dung) but nevertheless, indeed precisely so, *gains* Christ and is *found* in him. In the relationship in question it is intrinsically a matter of *dikaiosynē* (righteousness), of the question as to the proper, just, correct condition of man—namely, before God. In its relation to v. 9a the passage is remarkable because it is one of the few[1] in which the two lines of Pauline thought, which Lüdemann[2] in his day distinguished as the physico-mystical and the ethico-juridical concepts of redemption in Paul—the idea of *unio* (union) and of *justificatio* (justification)—obviously *meet*, and the second appears as the complement of the first. It is, of course, not Paul's *intention* to show that Christ's life in *him*, his life in *Christ*, is *dikaiosynē* (righteousness). But what

[1] Gal. 2.19 ff. could here also be mentioned.
[2] Cf. H. Lüdemann, *Die Anthropologie des Apostels Paulus*, 1872.

he now wants to do is to express in the ethico-juridical categories the fact that he cannot by any means exist as *en sarki pepoithōs* (relying on flesh), but in fact exists as a *beggar* and is rich only as such.

But the fact that v. 9b forms syntactically an interpretation of the *kerdēsō kai heurethō* (to gain Christ and be found in him) must now surely be of material significance too. If *dikaiosynē* (righteousness) were a condition such that man were in a position to place and maintain himself in it, if there were thus a *dikaiosynē* in front of which the word *emē, my* righteousness, could properly speaking be placed, if man could exist as *dikaios* (righteous) by keeping the Law *himself*—then what Paul has just described as his condition, and will describe further in vv. 10-11, would obviously also be something similar to what the Christian supporters of the Jewish religion sought to commend to their fellow-Christians. The idea that in addition to what one has to do as a Christian, in addition to the believing relationship to Christ (which of course was certainly not disparaged by the *kynes*—dogs—etc., of v. 2), in order to increase one's own righteousness and improve one's self-produced condition, it was necessary to *add* this and that from what the Jewish religion had to offer on these lines—that idea (and it was in fact the idea of the opponents attacked in this chapter) could not then be very far away. It is far from me, says Paul, because the believing relationship to Christ altogether excludes any thought of a *dikaiosynē* (righteousness) in which I have to place myself or assert myself, any thought of a righteousness of my own (*idia dikaiosynē*, Rom. 10.3), because Christ is at once the *end* of all religion, including any sort of *Christian* religion. For parallel to the *emēn* (my righteousness) he sets *tēn ek nomou.* 'Righteousness from the Law' means: righteousness from the religion that rests on revelation, righteousness as man—to be sure, on the basis of revelation—can have, practise and apply it. Thus, genuine religious righteousness. But (and this is what the *emēn* and the *ek nomou* have in common), *human* righteousness. In so far as belief in Christ is identical with disbelief in *this* righteousness, Christ is the end of the Law, the end—i.e. the thorough *relativizing*—of all religion over against its *Object*. And thus: it is not in virtue of '*my* righteousness, the righteousness from the *Law*',

that I *gain* Christ and am *found* in him, that *he is in me and I in him*—
that would be a contradiction in terms—but through *faith* in Christ.

The best way to understand the word *pistis* (faith), which bears
the emphasis here, is to notice that in the explanation of the *tēn dia
pisteōs* ([righteousness] *by faith*) Paul presently sets parallel to it the
expression *tēn ek theou* ([righteousness] *from God*)—that is, to make
pistis as little as possible a definition of human action by man
himself, and place the whole emphasis on the *Object* that is the
ground of *pistis*, in other words, on what takes place in *pistis*: the
determination, illumination, qualification of man by *God* or
Christ. If we operate too much here with trust, confidence, faithfulness, etc., on man's part towards God, then we almost inevitably come imminently near to the very thing that Paul wanted
his concept to abrogate and replace—man's own 'righteousness
from the Law'—and fail to understand the sharpness of the opposition he maintains towards it. Our 'own righteousness' could
indeed also consist in our surpassing everything else that can supposedly be done in this direction by now also believing, trusting,
etc., with all our heart. The decisive thing in the concept of faith
is of all things not the variously coloured psychological *capaci-
ties* which the believer discovers in himself and whose subject
he himself is, neither the animation nor the ardour of faith, neither
its rapture nor its repose—although in fact faith will always have
something of these and similar characteristics. On the contrary,
the decisive thing in all that is the absolute *limit* of all psychological capaciousness, the *limit* of his subjectivity, to which the
believer as such is brought—that limit which in fact is designated
(and that is why *dia pisteōs* stands parallel with *ek theou*) only by
the word *theos* (God) in all its salutary severity, the limit at which
man, confronted by the Personality, the Subjectivity of God,
knows himself for *lost*, and can know himself for righteous only
as *lost—gives himself up*, and can *take comfort* in the righteousness of
God only in this his self-surrender. *Perieram, nisi periissem* (I
would have perished, if I had not 'perished') is Calvin's description of this believing righteousness—and later: *fides offert nudum
hominem deo* (man is completely naked when faith offers him to
God). From man's point of view, faith in its decisive act is the

collapse of *every* effort of his own capacity and will, and the recognition of the absolute *necessity* of that collapse. In it he is truly lost. If man sees the *other* aspect: that as lost he is *righteous*, that in *giving* himself *up* he can *take comfort* in God's righteousness, then he sees himself—but it is *ek theou* (from God) that this vision comes—from God's point of view. That *happens* in faith. That *is* the positive thing that happens in faith. But precisely *this* happening, this *positive* thing in faith is not then the act of the human but of the originally *divine* faith. For it is not in virtue of the human but in virtue of the *divine* faithfulness that what man in faith knows to be true and real *is* in fact so—that God with *his* righteousness takes the lost creature's part, that the latter *as* lost is righteous. Thus the righteousness, integrity, correctness of man does not become a psychological capacity. It *remains* in God's hand. It is to be sought and found there, not here. It is and remains the righteousness of *Christ*, righteousness *ek theou* (from God). Transformation into *emē*, into an *idia dikaiosynē* (into 'my', into an 'own righteousness'), into a *justitia essentialis* (a righteousness inherent in [man's] nature), or the infusion of such a righteousness, does *not* take place. For the understanding of the concept *pistis* (faith) everything depends on whether the supposed Object, God, is understood as in fact the effecting Subject. To believe means to apprehend God and go on repeatedly apprehending God in *his* righteousness as the acting Subject, to give God the *glory* in self-surrender. Only when it is so understood does the nature of the opposition in which Paul here speaks become plain. Only so is it clear that he really has no intention of supplanting the Pharisaism of works by the far worse Pharisaism of the heart, of the inward nature, of the Christian mind, of the conscience one with God. To be religious in the Spirit of God and glory in Christ Jesus, and *pepoithenai en sarki* (to rely on flesh), exclude each other in fact all along the line. 'Before the world and apart from thy judgment it may well be musk, velvet and a piece of gold, but before thee, Lord, let me be an old cloth or rag with which I may wipe thy Son's shoes' (Luther).[1] There is no bridge between the one and the other. Here it is either-or. And it is just because

---

[1] Quoted in *Luthers Epistelnauslegung*, edited by Chr. G. Eberle, 1866, p. 697.

the believing relationship to Christ, precisely as a *believing* relationship, has this exclusiveness that alongside the *kerdainein Christon*
and *heurethēnai en autō* (the gaining Christ and being found in him)
there is *no* room for the works of the Jewish religion as well.

After the participial clause (v. 9b), which depends on the *hina*
clause (v. 9a), there now appears, *alongside* the *hina* clause, and
parallel to it in its dependence on the principal clause *hēgoumai
skybala* (I consider it dung, v. 8b), an infinitive clause (10): **in
order to know him**—to that end I hold all that I have and am as
a good Israelite to be 'dung'. The very boundary, the *limit* on this
side of which I can understand myself only as lost, is my connexion with him.[1] Notice, however, the remarkable order in
which the next expressions stand. At this limit it is a question of
knowing **the power of his resurrection.** Because he knows
him, Christ, and in particular the power of his resurrection,
because he will not and cannot fall from that knowledge—*therefore* he must on this side of the limit consider everything 'dung'.
But now the second thing Paul knows as a result of the power of
Christ's resurrection is not at all, as we might well expect, some
sort of happy change that befalls him, an exaltation and glorifica-
tion, but on the contrary: **the fellowship of his sufferings.** To
know Easter means, for the person knowing it, as stringently as
may be: to be implicated in the events of Good Friday—**to enter
into the form of his death,** or whatever may be the translation
of the sinister *symmorphizesthai*. The way in which the power of
Christ's resurrection works powerfully in the apostle is, that he is
clothed with the *shame of the Cross.* Thus his 'considering it all
dung' is far from being, say, only something in the nature of a
painful preliminary, a catharsis, a *via negativa*, a mystical emptying, which would afterwards the more surely be followed by an
uplift, a replenishment, a beatific vision and enjoyment. It is
rather the necessary and immutable expression of the *gnōsis
Christou Iēsou*, of the *kerdainein auton* and the *heurethēnai en autō*
(of the knowledge of Christ Jesus, of the gaining Christ and the

[1] *Gnōnai* (to know), as the sequel shows, here stretches far beyond a mere
exercise of the intellect.

being found in him). The power of Christ's resurrection brings about the dying of the apostle. It throws him back behind the limit of which we spoke, and sets on his life the stamp of the *earthly, human life of this world,* whose mark is *suffering,* whose formative power is *death.* True, it is the suffering and the death of Christ, who in his resurrection has proved himself the *Lord* of death. It is to him, to *his* death that Paul knows himself subject, not to nature, not to fate, not to *phthora* (decay) in themselves. Yet it is to his *death,* and that is the point here. Calvin's interpretation is rigorous, but true to the text: *Huc igitur comparatos esse nos omnes convenit, ut tota vita nostra nihil quam mortis imaginem repraesentet, donec mortem ipsam pariat. Sicuti vita Christi nihil aliud fuit quam mortis praeludium* (Our whole life must present nothing else but a picture of death, until it brings forth death itself. Just as *the life of Christ was nothing else but a prelude to his death*). *Pathēmata* and *thanatos Christou* (Christ's sufferings and death) stand here in contrast to the *kerdē* (gains) listed in vv. 5–6, to the *dikaiosynē emē* (my righteousness) of v. 9 and to everything in which it is possible to put fleshly confidence, in the same way as the *apothnēskein syn Christō* (dying with Christ) of Col. 2.20 f. stands in contrast to the *philosophia* and the *dogmatizesthai* (the 'philosophy' and the 'law-making') of the false teachers there. The death of Christ, into which those that are his were baptized (Rom. 6.4; Col. 2.12) and with which they are stamped by the power of his resurrection, is the death of everything in which it is possible to place such confidence—or to put it more precisely: the death of the man who is capable of such confidence. Thrown back in principle within the bounds of his fleshly nature thus marked, he has nothing— absolutely nothing—left to him, risen with Christ as he is, except to 'seek what is above where Christ is' (Col. 3.1). *That* is why the believing relationship is so exclusive (v. 9). *That* is why Paul must consider everything else dung. In v. 11 he goes on to speak, hesitatingly and cautiously at first, of this one remaining possibility.

In the hope that so—i.e. as *symmorphizomenos tō thanatō autou* (by entering into the form of his death, v. 10)—**I may be on the way to the resurrection of the dead.** *That* is what is left when everything else has been surrendered with Christ to death and recognized as shame and disgrace: the mortifying power of the resurrection *itself*. It is indeed this power, as the power of *Christ's* resurrection, that determines, conditions and surrounds the apostle's situation as described in v. 10. In that he *places* himself in this situation, *knows* himself placed in it, the resurrection appears on the edge of his *own* horizon. Exerting *fatal* power on this side of the horizon—but *visible* as *resurrection*! Without it, without the risen Christ, Paul could still *pepoithenai en sarki* (rely on flesh). That possibility is taken from him by the Risen One, who is indeed none other than the Crucified One and who as such has made himself known to him as the Lord (vv. 8, 10). But precisely in its being taken from him—by his inclusion in the fellowship of his *sufferings*, by his entry into the form of his *death*—he is undeniably also *given* the hope of his own resurrection. 'If we are dead with Christ, we believe that we shall also *live* with him' (Rom. 6.8)—*synzēsomen!* That is the hope! And therefore here *katantēsō*. This *katantan* accordingly does not mean stepping out of the situation of v. 10, but *in* that situation stepping courageously and assuredly towards its end—stretching out (as it will be put later) towards the very thing that makes it so dreadful, because precisely that is the thing that holds the key to its meaning and the solution of its mystery. He who *kills* is also he who makes *alive*. So, and only so—by *assenting* to his killing—are we on the way to life.

Such then, says Paul in vv. 4-11, pointing to his own person by way of example—such is the condition of man when he lives in the manner of the new, true people of God, considering himself no longer religious except through the Spirit of God, no longer able to glory except in Christ Jesus, no longer able to rely on flesh. He does not live as if he had found a new bridge from here to the beyond, from man to God, from destruction to redemption—a new bridge alongside of which the old one could then very well be used again too on occasion. On the contrary, he lives in the knowledge that there is *no* bridge from here to *there*, but solely the way from there to *here*—the way that from beginning to end and all along is *God's* way. I consider that there is no reason why vv. 12 ff., to which we now turn, should not also be understood in this context. They do not involve any break, as if in the foregoing

Paul had sought to paint his unity with Christ 'on the heights of inspiration' (Lueken), but now returned soberly and soberingly to the assurance: nevertheless even I have not yet wholly grasped Christ but am still on the way, or whatever paraphrase is preferred. As if after all that was said in vv. 7-11 there were need of such a reservation! As if it were not much simpler to take vv. 12 ff. as a development of what was last said—'in the hope that so I may be on the way to the resurrection of the dead'—as a picture of his relation to Christ as it now determines his present attitude, now that he has been thrown off the Pharisaic track. Thus v. 11 leads straight on to v. 12:

Not as if I had already apprehended or had already reached the goal. That corresponds to the 'not with my righteousness from the Law' of v. 9. Notice first of all in general that Paul would here compare his life to a contest in the stadium. Similarly in 2.16 above, and also I Thess. 5.15; I Cor. 9.24; I Tim. 6.11 f.; II Tim. 4.7. His predilection for *this* picture is very closely connected with the Pauline struggle for the righteousness of God. One would expect differently. The man who knows only a *dikaiosynē ek theou* (a righteousness from God) and God only as *Subject*, will surely know only of a life of passivity. That is the one thing of which Paul knows *nothing at all*. On the contrary, he knows only of a life of greatest activity—in view of this verse one might almost say, most hectic activity. To lose confidence in the flesh, to give God alone the glory—*that* means concretely, to know what it is to be committed, unresting, intent, out to win. If there is one man who knows *no* passivity, then it is the *symmorphizomenos tō thanatō Christou* (the man who enters into the form of Christ's death).

But that is not what Paul wishes to say and to show the basis for here. That he is a 'runner', and why, is a thing he does not by this time need to tell the Philippians. It is self-evident that in *that* respect he does not come behind the champions of the Law. But he would not care to see his 'running' confused with theirs. Not because he sets *greater* store by his, but because he sets *less* store by it. The way of our own righteousness consists step by step in an ever-increasing *apprehension*. Each stage of the way is at once also a goal. We become, we grow, we acquire, we appropriate, we become ever more devout, ever purer, ever surer. Our own righteousness is like a capital that bears compound interest, however small it may be. Admittedly the process must go on, admittedly we are 'not yet wholly' perfect. But what is the meaning of 'not yet wholly'? Then there is no danger: all sorts of heights, possessions, potential gains, personal perfections nevertheless appear to have been already attained. How remarkable that it has been found possible to expound the present passage as if Paul, too, had now wanted merely to make the harmless remark that in course of such a process he had admittedly not yet reached the goal, but was nevertheless, like the people of Kierkegaard's Copenhagen, making *progressus infinitus* (infinite progress) towards it. If he had seen it that way, he would certainly *not* have been able to split with the Jewish Christians. They too could have spoken of 'striving ever to high endeavour', and Paul for his part could then quite well have conceded that a touch of Jewish legalism in the way it is done is also permissible on occasion. But his argument here is of a different kind: it does not deny the necessity of running, and in fact racing for the goal of perfection, but rather asserts it. It roundly denies, however, the idea that there is anything we thereby attain, apprehend or get behind us. *Ouch...ēdē* does not mean 'not yet wholly', but 'not yet'. That we have *not yet* apprehended, have *not yet* reached the goal, not even in part, applies to the Christian position *in principle*. It is best *not* to supply the object of *elabon* (have apprehended)—neither by 'it', nor by 'Christ', and certainly not by 'righteousness'. The *tertium comparationis* is the athlete as he speeds on with outstretched, empty hands. Not until v. 14 is there mention of the *brabeion* (prize), and we shall hear how.

I race on in the hope that I may apprehend. That must first of all be taken entirely on its own. The Christian 'not yet' accordingly does not by any means appear to be a check or a sedative. The fundamental 'not yet' itself calls to mind inescapably an equally fundamental 'then'. The *ei kai* (in the hope that I may apprehend) is to be compared with the *ei pōs* of v. 11 (in the hope that so I may be on the way to the resurrection of the dead). And it is the same thing that is at stake here as there. Paul would be understood as one who with head held high steps—no, it is now put much more strongly: races on—towards the horizon, but (and this is the point of the present passage) *only* as such, not at all as one who has already apprehended, altogether only as one who stretches out in unspeakable longing towards apprehension.

But if that is the Christian position, is it not a terrible void? Can we exist like that? *Eph' hō*, Paul answers, **seeing that I am apprehended by Christ Jesus.** We interpret that in the light of the foregoing verse: seeing that he has made himself known to me as Lord, that his righteousness never again lets go of me in faith, that the power of his resurrection has placed me in the fellowship of his sufferings. Seeing that is so, in view of this happening of which *he* is the one and only Subject, I run and am well content to be *only* a runner, a *viator* and not a *comprehensor* (a wanderer and not an apprehender), content *not* to have apprehended, content to stretch out *empty* hands. To *be* apprehended is enough. It requires no correlative on my side, and can have none. The incomprehensible divine *constraint* is enough—I must, in view of the *anō klēsis* (the calling valid above) of v. 14. Because it is *divine* constraint, it means *per se* (of itself) not only must but also may, can and will. Seeing that is so, I race on. The sentimental question whether that is endurable, whether it is not an empty risk, a leap into the dark, is not considered at all, is settled in advance—seeing that I am apprehended by Christ Jesus. That is the substance, fulness, possession, joy, assurance—all in him who 'apprehends' Paul, and *seeing that is so*, in the Paul who *is* 'apprehended' by him. And *his*, Paul's hands remain empty thereby! Not, only half full, but—empty! *Not* as if I had already apprehended.

13-14.   Brothers, I consider myself not to have already apprehended. *Oupo* (*not . . .* already) is to be joined with *kateilēphenai* (have comprehended), not with *logizomai* (consider). The suggestion that Paul should one day consider the idea in question is surely of no importance. Paul is obviously answering in v. 13 an expected objection. The readers want to cry out: but you are Paul, the apostle, you really *have* already 'apprehended' a great deal, you really *have* already reached many goals, at least provisional ones. Don't paint it too black, don't think too humbly, too pessimistically of yourself! But it is not a question of humility or pessimism. Paul could in other contexts take a very vigorous stand on his rights, his knowledge, his work, his dignity, his successes. But not in *this* context. *Logizomai*: I consider, I reckon, I judge that I have *not* already apprehended. Everything I have apprehended falls right out of my hands the moment I think of how I stand before Christ, of how I stand in Christ before God.

Hen de: **One thing however is true,** positively and decisively true in this estimate, this fundamental assessment of his situation: **forgetting what is behind** (not looking back any more on the part of the course that lies behind me, not thinking any more of what has already been achieved, apprehended, appropriated), **stretching out to what lies ahead, I race towards the goal.** Here the significance of the picture reaches its height: what is behind! what lies ahead! forgetting the former, stretching out to the latter! Man in between as the point where the decision is made, as the pivot of the great inversion, not making up his own mind but having his mind made up, not turning himself the other way round but being turned the other way round, not himself moving but *agomenos pneumati theou* (driven by the Spirit of God, Rom. 8.14). *That* is Paul. *That* is how he considers himself. 'The prize', however, for which he runs (it is still not 'apprehended'!) is—and now comes the last astonishing thought in this astonishing paragraph—*hē anō klēsis tou theou en Christō Iēsou*. I venture the translation: **the divine calling in Christ Jesus which is valid above.** He runs (be it noted, in the situation of v. 10!) seeing that he is apprehended by Christ Jesus (v. 12). He is called. To be true to this calling is both his task and his reward as well. Really his reward as well? Yes, and that too not because the calling also means promise, hope of resurrection, hope of glory—it does, but that is not expressly mentioned in v. 14—but because it is valid *above*, because it is *divine* calling, because it has taken place in *Jesus Christ*. *This* calling is glory, it is rewarding for its own sake. He who has the *anō klēsis* (the calling valid above)[1] cannot

[1] Dibelius thinks *klēsis* (calling) must be understood as if Paul had written *doxa* (glory). There is something in that, for indeed v. 11 had spoken of 'being on the way to the resurrection of the dead'. But it is surely no accident that what is 'above', absolutely above (in the same Beyond as could in itself also be denoted by *exanastasis tōn nekrōn*—resurrection of the dead—or by *doxa*), is

ask: what will become of me in all this? He knows that possessing *this* he is rich in all his boundless poverty.

With that the great antithesis of vv. 4-14 comes to a close. We must not overlook the singularity of the picture given, but still less, if we follow the text at any rate, may we simply observe that and no more. Paul's autobiographical passages, here as in chapter 1, as also in Gal. 1; II Cor. 11-12; Rom. 7, are by no means an end in themselves. Not of course that they are mere incidentals either. They are in fact fully valid model illustrations of the truth as Paul states it. In the conditions under which *he* exists, the readers are to perceive the conditions under which they *themselves* exist. In the picture of his situation they are to see reflected the principles of the Christian situation in general, and realize that they cannot break through them. That is what was intended in vv. 4-14.

In vv. 15 ff. we have the application *ad hominem* of what was said in vv. 4-14, a summons by Paul to the Philippians to persevere with him in this situation as the true Christian one, and not suffer themselves to be forced into a different relation to God by the propaganda in question. We must not let ourselves be deceived here, especially by v. 19, into thinking that Paul now suddenly turns to another front, i.e. to attack the moral laxity of certain Christians (Lueken). No—those whose God is the belly, whose glory is in their shame and who mind earthly things are again, in all too drastic terms, the *Jewish Christians* against whose influence the whole chapter seeks to give warning. The decisive description of those Paul is attacking in vv. 15 ff. is really the one given in v. 18: they are **enemies of the Cross of Christ.** What that means can be learned from I Cor. 1.23 and Gal. 6.12, and it is not possible to see how the concept should here suddenly be given

here called *klēsis*, the demand and promise that sets the elect in motion here on earth. This *klēsis* (calling) has come from above, is valid above, has above its truth, its legitimacy, its meaning, just as according to Col. 3.3 the Christians' life is hidden in God. This *klēsis* (calling) and the *brabeion* (prize) are one and the same. If Paul had written *doxa* (glory), then the thought would not be ruled out that he promised himself some reward for his running *besides* the fact that the risen Christ in setting him in motion is *himself* his reward both here and beyond —that is, that his running had again after all the character of a *work* directed towards an effect. That, however, is the very thought which in this paragraph he particularly wishes to rule out.

a specifically moral meaning—quite apart from the havoc caused
to the coherence of the chapter when Paul, having like as not
been made to wander from the point already in vv. 12 ff., is now
from v. 15 or v. 17 on suddenly made to attack ethical libertines
as well. No—vv. 15 ff. form the continuation, or rather properly
speaking the consummation, of the warning that began with the
threefold *blepete* (beware) in v. 2.

15.   Because Paul has in vv. 4-14 given the ground of this warning in the form of a presentation of his own situation, he can now
go on and sum up the whole argument in an exhortation which is
at first sight startling, but in view of what has been said so far is
not really startling at all: be followers of me (v. 17). First of all he
puts it in a different way: **We, then, who are perfect, let us
think on that!** *Teleioi* (perfect) is obviously a slogan or catch-
word, perhaps the very one used by the opposition party with
their eagerness for Christians to perform special actions and be in
a special moral and ritual state. Possibly the *teteleiōmai* of v. 12
(Luther [and AV] translate it: 'were already perfect') is already an
allusion to that. Christian perfection, Paul now tells them, consists in being in the *same* condition and adopting the *same* attitude
as he wrote of himself in vv. 4-14. It consists, stated paradoxically,
in Christian *imperfection*, in *running* towards the goal, in knowing
that the salvation of the Christian and his heavenly calling are one
and the same. By the first *touto* (that) in v. 15 we have to understand: the meaning of the Christian position as evinced in the life
of Paul. The sequel runs: **And if you wish to think differently
about anything, then God will give you revelation also in
that.** This translation, of course, already contains an interpretation of the strangely prolix sentence. What is the meaning of
heterōs phronein? What does Paul mean when he says in the
second clause literally: 'this also God will reveal to you'? I try to
understand it as follows: Paul grants that it is also possible to
think differently from him about the things designated by the
first *touto*—*heterōs*, not differently in any *intrinsic* sense, but in
form and *expression*, that is, in the comprehension of the Christian
position, in the understanding of its meaning—whereby, however,

it should be noticed that there is no getting rid of a note of disapproval in the word *heterōs* (differently). And he now expresses the hope that in such divergencies (that would thus be what is meant by the second *touto*) 'the rectification from God's side through the operation of revelation will not fail to come' (Meyer). A question mark still remains here for me.

16.   Only, let us continue in the direction in which we have come! Paul knows himself with the Philippians on *one* path which, so far at least, has in principle taken the direction described in vv. 4-14. The possibility of a *heterōs phronein* about the first *touto* (that is, of 'thinking differently about that') is reserved, except that it cannot mean any divergence from the path itself. On in this direction!—no extravagances to right or to left! That is the meaning of *tō autō stoichein* (to continue in the same direction). *Dei* has to be supplied with this infinitive, as in Rom. 12.15.

And now v. 17. **Be followers of me, brothers, and watch those who walk according to the example you have in us!** That refers, unless we are determined to see a new thought appearing most abruptly here, once more to what Paul has said of himself: considering as loss, as dung, all that the flesh could take comfort in—*no* righteousness of my own—*not as if* I had already apprehended—*forgetting* what is behind—racing on to the *skopos* (goal)! That is how Paul walks, and that, as is not unknown to the readers, is how others walk with him. It is surely plain that the demand, 'Be followers of me!', is in *that* context not only bearable but wholly to the point. What is to be seen in *him*, Paul, as a Christian is in point of fact not anything positive on which *he* could pride himself, but *Christ*—that is, however, the traces of the *dynamis tēs anastaseōs autou* (the power of his resurrection), the fellowship of his sufferings, a *gap* so to speak, a lack, a defect: he is *not* holy, *not* righteous, *not* perfect, all for the sake of Christ. This *typos* (example) he can really without presumptuousness commend to them for imitation. But why does he do it just here?

18 supplies the answer: **For many walk, whom I have often described to you, but now describe in tears as enemies of the Cross of Christ.** Would it not be remarkable if the reference to earlier warnings (*hous pollakis elegon hymin*) which at once recalls v. 1, and the revival of the heated outburst of v. 2 (*nyn de kai klaiōn legō*, but now describe in tears), should here suddenly point in a totally different direction? And 'the Cross of Christ' is, according to the parallels already cited, the strongest expression for the radical opposition of Christian truth not so much to moral licence and the pursuit of earthly, sensual pleasure, as rather to the religious and ethical presumptuousness that seeks to achieve what man is utterly incapable of achieving, what can only be given to him in faith. Those who would seek to get round this barrier,[1] who resist the power of Christ's resurrection that seeks to drive them into the fellowship of his sufferings, who will *not* walk the way of poverty described in vv. 4-14, the way of being for Christ's sake *not* holy, *not* righteous, *not* perfect—these are 'enemies of the Cross of Christ'. For whoever here seeks a different way, seeks the opposite. Neutrality is here excluded.

19 supplies four further definitions, to understand which we must think back to the biting polemic of v. 2. There it was: *unclean*—in your cleanness! *evil* workers—in your zeal! *mutilation* with your circumcision! They expect a part in the Messianic Kingdom, in God and in his glory, on the ground of their piety—no, answers Paul: **their end is destruction!**—in the Messianic judgment they will not stand. **Their God the belly and their glory in their shame!**—a further allusion to circumcision which for concreteness leaves nothing to be desired. Finally: **who set their minds on earthly things**—a paraphrase of what in v. 3 he had called *pepoithenai en sarki* (relying on flesh). That we are not to think of earthly-mindedness in a *materialistic* sense is shown by the meaning which *phronein ta epi tēs gēs* (to set the mind on earthly things) also has in the context of Col. 3.2. What makes the passage so pregnant is precisely the fact that Paul takes the most exalted religious and ethical austerity of those he would warn against and describes it in terms which in fact, if they were found

---

[1] *Grenzpfahl*, lit. boundary post: the Cross is here likened to a post or pole that stands, like a 'halt sign' at the frontier, to mark the limit of human endeavour (*Translator*).

in any other context would have to be understood as a description of common fleshly sins. That, however, is *intentional*. That is how Jewish-Christian piety really does look, seen from the standpoint of the preaching of the Cross, and this joint view of the most exalted righteousness and basest sin must *not* be obliterated by adopting the usual interpretation that Paul is here speaking of depravity. Of course he is speaking of depravity, but the fact that he brands as depraved those who, bypassing the Cross of Christ and bypassing faith and its righteousness, call for *holiness* and *cleanness*—that he drags their *glory* in the mire (he may well and truly do it, after having done exactly the same with his own glory in vv. 7 ff.)—*that* is the bitter point of vv. 15 ff.

20a, which is comparable to the *hēmeis gar esmen* (for we are [the circumcision]) of v. 3, brings once more the Christian antithesis, generalizing what Paul had given in vv. 8-10 as the aim of his own life: **For our citizenship is in heaven.** *En ouranois* (in heaven)—it is on that that the accent falls. In contrast to those described in vv. 18-19 as 'enemies of the Cross of Christ' who set their minds on *ta epigeia* (earthly things), the Christians have the object of their attachment *in heaven*—i.e. as is plain from the whole context, not in their hands, not present, not in their power. *Standing* in the truth that is established in the world by the Cross of Christ means standing in this *antithesis*, in the 'Now' that is not yet the 'One day', in the 'Here' that is not yet the 'Beyond', seeking what is *above*, knowing one's life hidden with Christ in God. Paul calls the object of the Christians' attachment their *politeuma*.[1] It is the constitution or *judicial order* which is authoritative for us, which is to be appealed to by us, which protects us, and accordingly in that sense our 'citizenship'. The question of the judicial order which at once both obliges and protects men is in

[1] Dibelius points out an interesting special meaning of this word: 'A colony of foreigners whose organization mirrors the home *politeia* on a small scale and which is accordingly called after it.' But if Paul had been using the word in this special sense, then it would obviously be just the life of Christians here and now that he would have had to call a *politeuma*, and relegate their *politeia* to heaven. It will therefore be advisable here (as with the corresponding verb *politeuesthai*, 'to be in a state', which occurs in 1.27) to abide by the meaning nearest to hand.

fact the point at issue in this whole chapter. Whether *ek nomou* or *dikaiosynē ek theou* (righteousness from the Law or from God)—that (v. 9) is the question. And the *politeuma en ouranois* (citizenship in heaven) is now obviously only another expression for the latter.[1] We—and that is the urgent thing which according to v. 1 he is determined not to tire of writing to the Philippians—we stand under *God's* righteousness, and so now: under the righteousness established in heaven. It is *his* judicial order that obliges us and protects us. Further—it is not conditioned by our wishes and capabilities, but is unconditionally grounded in itself. Further—it is not imagination but reality. All that is contained in the *en ouranois* (in heaven). *That* is what Paul strives for, here as also against the false teachers of Colossians. The *eschatological* determination of the antithesis has in these later Epistles, as compared with Galatians and Romans, become more striking and more obvious. More than that I should not like to say.

20b-21 provide once more a positive comment on the Christian truth which has been the motive force of this delimitation, the nerve of this polemic chapter: **From there** (from heaven) **we expect also the Deliverer, the Lord Jesus Christ, who will change our body in its humiliation into the form of his body in its glory, by means of the power with which he can subdue everything to himself.** It is the thought of v. 11 that here reappears in generalized form. *Hence* all the repudiation, negation, aloofness, tension, that is so characteristic of the Pauline polemic. *Hence* the ruthless, inexorable suppression of the religious man with his aspirations and illusions. *Hence* the picture that in its outward aspect is again and again so incomprehensible, so provoking, so offensive particularly to the religious man—the picture of the Christian position as it is drawn for us especially in vv. 12-14: race track, forgetting everything that is behind, stretching out empty hands in front, *everything* positive out there ahead, up there above, at the goal—*hēmōn to politeuma en ouranois* (our citizenship in heaven). *Hence* righteousness *dia pisteōs, ek theou*

---

[1] *Dikaiosynē* is already in Gal. 5.5 equivalent to *elpis dikaiosynēs*, an object of the same *apekdechesthai* as here the *sōtēr* who comes from heaven.

(by faith, from God). Why? Because the Christian expects *less* of
God than does the other with his programme and his method of
cultivating the new life? No, but because he expects more.
Because his God is not an abstraction, not an object, not an
opposite number, because his God is really and immediately
present to the reality of man in the concrete sense—to man as
sōma (body), which we know only as *sōma tapeinōseōs* (humilia-
tion-body). *That*, the existence of man as the being that as Adam's
child he is—fallen, humiliated, limited, qualified, abandoned to
phthora (decay)—*that* is the question that oppresses us. Man himself is the question to which man must have an answer. What the
others seek and preach in place of faith, means forgetting and
overlooking that question. It is not a new and improved kind of
morality and religion that God has given in Christ, but an answer
to *that* question. We wait for the *Deliverer* Jesus Christ. The
supreme attribute of the figure of the *sōtēr* (deliverer) in the religious idealogy of that time was just this: that he is the bringer of
the *life* that man lacks. But whence do we await the Deliverer?
From the realm of the spirit and the spirits, from the realm of the
abstractions and ideals which are man's *own* reflected image and
to which as a logical consequence man himself is able to secure his
admittance? But anyone able to take comfort in such a deliverer
as that does not *wait* for him, but *has* him already. Really? A
deliverer who delivers him, extricates him, frees him, quickens
him, makes him a new creature? He does not then *believe* either,
nor does he need to believe—i.e. to depend wholly and completely on God's *own* righteousness. However humbly he may
behave, he has in fact both hands full. Even his humility, his consciousness of sin or his mystical self-emptying are riches. He does
not expect, he already possesses. Why? Because he knows nothing of the real question and the real answer. Because he assuredly
does *not* know the *sōtēr*, the Saviour as the Bringer of Life. Else he
would unreservedly *await* him, and in fact await him *from heaven*,
and in fact await him as the One who will change our body in its
humiliation. Into what? Into the form of his body in its glory—
that is, into his, the new heavenly Adam's, form of existence,
which is positively the end of all things. Each word here is

important and significant. With the same power that the *kyrios* (the Lord) uses in order to make *ta panta* (all things) subject to himself and through him to the Father, he will transform us, make us new. Us? Yes, us who, praising him here and now as the *kyrios, wait* for the revelation of his *kyriotēs* (lordship). We wait for our inclusion in this his one indivisible, divine, sovereign act which comprehends at once both the living and the dead. We wait, content that the *klēsis* (calling) thereto, which promises this our inclusion, has taken place and is valid (v. 14). That is the *sōtēria*, the thoroughgoing salvation, which the Cross *marks* in the world as near at hand *but also* sharply and fundamentally *distinguishes* from all shallow pseudo-deliverances. Whoever *pneumati theou latreuei* (is religious through the Spirit of God, v. 3), *waits*. According to vv. 12-14 one can equally well say: he *hastens*. As one who waits he hastens, giving God the glory, towards the *kyrios Iēsous Christos* (the Lord Jesus Christ), who *himself* will make *all things* new. That—the resurrection of the dead and the Christian hope—is the positive thing that Paul has been contending for in this chapter.

1 of chapter 4[1] belongs as an adjuratory conclusion to chapter 3.[2] **Therefore my brothers, my beloved for whom I long, my joy and my crown, stand fast like that in the Lord, my beloved!** The personal importunacy of these words speaks for itself. The imperative *stēkete* (stand fast) reminds us of 1.27, where the first great exhortation of the letter (1.27-2.16) opened with the same demand as now closes the second (3.2-4.1). The description of the readers as *stephanos mou* (my crown) reminds us of 2.16, where he called them his 'glory against the day of Jesus Christ', and of the similar expressions in I Thess. 2.19; II Cor. 1.14. It is one of the most intimate touches in Paul, which we understand when it begins to dawn on us how he hopes to stand then—then, in the great Then of the fulfilment—adorned by those whom in their hasting and waiting he has brought, as has now once more happened, to the Lord, presenting to the *kyrios* his *ekklēthentes*, to the Lord his elect, to the Head his Body, the *coetus vocatorum* (circle of the called), the Church.

---

[1] The chapter division is mistaken here also, as at the end of chapter 2.
[2] Cf. I Cor. 15.58.

I urge Euodia and I urge Syntyche to mind the one thing in the
Lord. Yes, and I beg you also, good Synzygos, to help them;
they stood by me in the struggle for the Gospel, along with
Clement and my other fellow-workers, whose names stand in
the book of life. Rejoice in the Lord at all times! Once more I
say it: rejoice! May your benevolence be manifest to all men!
The Lord is near! Do not be anxious about anything, but as often
as you worship and pray let your troubles come before God
with thanksgiving, so will the peace of God, which surpasses all
understanding, guard your hearts and your thoughts in Christ
Jesus. Finally, brothers, whatever is true, whatever is honourable, whatever is righteous, whatever is pure, whatever is
kindly, whatever is praiseworthy, whatever is called a virtue
and deserves recognition—think on that! And what you have
learned and received and heard and seen in me—do that! So will
the God of peace be with you.

The mutual interconnexion between these verses is for us unrecognizable. There must have been a completely concrete link,
which we lack the means to reconstruct. Vv. 2-3 go along with
each other, and somewhat more loosely vv. 6-7 and vv. 8-9, while
in between v. 4, v. 5a, and v. 5b stand entirely on their own. It is a
handful of requests, hints, observations and encouragements that
Paul throws down before addressing himself to his last theme in
vv. 10 ff. The passage is for that very reason one of the liveliest
and most allusive in Paul, or anywhere at all in the New Testament.

**I urge Euodia and I urge Syntyche to mind the one thing
in the Lord.** First of all, then, a repetition of the exhortation to
unity that met us in one of the most central passages of the letter
(2.2), but now with special application to two female members of

the congregation. It is better to abide by this view and not have
the presumption to assume with the expositors of the Tübingen
school that (presupposing, of course, that the letter is not genuine)
we have to do with an allegory—Euodia and Syntyche being the
Jewish Christian and Gentile Christian parties, and the *synzygos*
of v. 3 (Synzygos thus = the Unifier) none other than the mediating apostle Peter! We hear of these women presently that 'in the
struggle for the Gospel', i.e. surely on the occasion of the founding
of the congregation as described in Acts 16, they had 'stood by'
Paul—a word of commendation such as is likewise conferred on
some Christian women in Rom. 16.12. What had now disunited
them, we do not know. It is sufficient that, as v. 3 shows, the very
memory of trouble shared in the cause makes it the apostle's care
to see them united again. As in 2.2, the only thing that may be
assumed with certainty is, that it was not merely some personal
squabble that Paul had in view in bidding them *to auto phronein*
(mind the one thing).

**Yes, and I beg you also, good Synzygos, to help them:
they stood by me in the struggle for the Gospel, along with
Clement and my other fellow-workers, whose names
stand in the book of life.** *Synzygos* means literally yoke-fellow,
companion. Older expositors, e.g. Clement of Alexandria and
Erasmus, have sought in the person so addressed another woman,
and in fact, despite I Cor. 7, the wife of Paul himself. But, as
Calvin rightly asks, *unde illi uxor Philippis?* (How should Paul suddenly have had a wife in Philippi of all places?). The subtle idea
that the *synzygos* was probably the husband of one of the two
women may likewise be left aside. Yet neither is the word, as
Luther thought in his translation, a title of honour conferred on
some Christian in Philippi who stood specially close to him, but
it is quite simply a male proper name, whose bearer to be sure is as
unknown to us as the two women he is to help, obviously by
mediating. Another who must also be listed as unknown is the
Clement whom Paul names as his fellow-worker along with
some others who are not named. Perhaps we are to gather from
the following clause that he and these *loipoi* (the other fellow-
workers) are already dead: their names stand in the book of life.

At all events the expression says: God *knows* them, and that too as righteous, as his own, like Euodia and Syntyche, like Clement. Perhaps Paul is after all speaking solely of people who are alive and the expression *hōn ta onomata.* . . . (whose names . . .) is a circumlocution for the whole congregation, whom he would thereby make responsible for settling the dispute in question. The book in which God has written the names of his own appears already in Ex. 32.32. In Ps. 69.28 it is called the 'book of the living'. We read in Isa. 4.3 of those left in Zion that are written among the living. According to Luke 10.20 the names of the disciples are written in heaven. And finally, the *biblion zōēs* (book of life) appears in Rev. 3.5; 13.8; 20.12. According to the wording or sense of these passages, it is *God* who enters men in this book. Thomas Aquinas and Calvin will be right when they relate this picture to the concept of *election*. One has the impression that Paul at the end of v. 3 has already—despite the syntactical and logical connexion—no longer in view only the admonition to the two women and the request to Synzygos, but that the reminder of the book of life in which the comrades in arms are entered from all eternity has at all events *also* (it is not unusual in Paul for the thought to shift like that) independent significance. If so, then to that extent the injunction that follows would not after all appear entirely out of the blue.

Rejoice in the Lord at all times! Once more I say it: rejoice! We met this summons already in 2.18, and then again at the close of the paragraph (3.1). Compare also 1.4; 1.18; 2.17. In the light of these passages, 'joy' in Philippians is a defiant 'Nevertheless!' which Paul sets like a full stop against the Philippians' *anxiety* (1.18 and 2.17-18) and their possible *displeasure* over Epaphroditus (3.1). Here in 4.4 there is no such antithesis to be found in the preceding clauses. We should accordingly have to look for it in what follows—which, however, would again mean in the Philippians' *merimnan* (being anxious) in v. 6. For the moment, it stands here entirely on its own—rejoice!—following on the reminder of the book of life, and isolating the keynote which Paul strikes in this letter. It is in fact as keynote that this joy is meant, beyond the joy that one 'has', feels, can show. *En kyriō* (in

the Lord) is its location; at all times it can and must take place.
It would be an empty phrase, were it not here too correlated with
the Christian hope, with the resurrection of the dead. It is, however, no empty phrase. In 1.18, too, the *chairō* (I rejoice) clearly
stands in *that* correlation. That is why it can also be expressed as an
imperative: to rejoice, to let ourselves be comforted, strengthened
and encouraged, is from the Christian point of view a command
like any other.

May your benevolence be manifest to all men! That is the
literal translation. But Luther's translation—'Let your lenity be
made known . . .'—perhaps comes nearer to the meaning after
all. *To epieikes* (for *hē epieikeia*) denotes a disposition that can
hardly be rendered in translation by a single word. It is your
quite specifically grounded benevolence, gentleness, considerate-
ness, openness, vitality and at the same time moderation (for that
reason it has also been translated *aequitas*) that must become
manifest to all men. Luther's 'lenity' (*Lindigkeit*) well expresses the
source of this disposition: Christians are men who have been
made *lenis*, lenient, mellow, 'beaten to pulp', as opposed to the
non-recipients of grace, who can still be stiff and bristly. The
treatment of Epaphroditus in 2.15 ff. may perhaps be recalled as
an example of what is meant. Is there a connexion with the preceding verse? Luther says:[1] before God be glad at all times, but
before men be lenient! Bengel sees a still closer connexion:
Gaudium in domino parit veram aequitatem (joy in the Lord begets
true equity). Perhaps there is also a link going back to the admonition to unity in v. 2, or forwards to v. 6: instead of being tempted
into anxiety by the pressure that is being put on you, rather let
the lenity which it should produce in you shine before men. This
result goes *along with* joy. And perhaps we are to think[2] at the
same time of the fact that the Lord is near: the time of rejoicing is
at the door—see that all men notice it! It will be best to take
account of *all* these connexions. One way or another everything
here is surely interconnected. The 'being manifest to all men'
makes us think of 2.15.

The Lord is near! Why joy? Why benevolence? The answer

[1] Works, Erlangen edn, 7.118.   [2] With Dibelius.

is given by a testimony to the great hope of the New Testament, whose content we heard something of in 3.20 f. Here we find its shortest formulation. He is near, whom we wait for to change our body (3.21). I should not say that the proximity of which Paul here speaks is simply the proximity of eternity to all time. For he is not speaking of eternity as such, but of the coming of the Lord who is the end of time as he is its beginning. The Christian, himself in time, looks forward to that end and therefore undoubtedly views it in terms of an interval of time, not merely in terms of the relation between time and eternity. But he finds that this interval, whatever happens, is *short*. Whether it be small or great, it is relativized, limited by the Lord who is its end. The Christian lives in time that is not yet suspended but thoroughly relativized, in time whose limit is known to him in Christ, not in an infinite world but in a finite one upheld at its beginning and its end by God. Calvin was in essence perfectly right, however unhistorical it appears at first sight, when in explaining this verse he spoke of the *fiducia providentiae divinae* (trust in divine providence). It is in the knowledge that 'the Lord is near' that Philippians was written, and it cannot be understood from any other standpoint.

Do not be anxious about anything, but as often as you worship and pray let your troubles come before God with thanksgiving. The 'anxiety' of which Paul speaks must not be understood merely in a general sense. It will not be for nothing that the *mēden* (not anything) is so strongly emphasized. We have seen how Paul in 1.12-26 and 2.17-3.1 wrestled with the Philippians' anxiety on his behalf. The accent of the sentence lies not on the fact that they are to *worship* and *pray*, nor on the fact that they are to lay their *aitēmata* (troubles) before *God*, but on the fact that they are to do both these things with *thanksgiving, meta eucharistias*. That accords with the tenor of 1.12 ff. and 2.17 ff. To begin by praising God for the fact that in *this* situation, as it is, he is so mightily God—such a beginning is the *end* of anxiety. To be anxious means that we ourselves suffer, ourselves groan, ourselves seek to see ahead. Thanksgiving means giving God the glory in everything, making room for him, casting our care on him,

letting it be his care. The troubles that exercise us then cease to be
hidden and bottled up. They are so to speak laid open towards
God, spread out before him.

**So will the peace of God, which surpasses all understand-
ing, guard your hearts and your thoughts in Christ Jesus.**
'Guard' is the (more pregnant!) translation, in place of 'keep'.
Man is *unguarded*, open to every enemy and every danger, as long
as he does not *give thanks*, as long as in all the worship and prayer
which he perhaps does not neglect, he still keeps his troubles to
himself, shut away from God, instead of presenting them to God,
revealing them to him as the *Lord* to whom his praises are due.
If he *does* do that—this may be the connexion between vv. 6 and
7[1]—then the peace of God guards his heart and his thoughts. It
is 'in Christ Jesus' that this guarding takes place. The peace of God
is the order and security of the kingdom of Christ among those
that are his. It can be asked if the peace of God denotes *the* peace
which God himself has and guarantees—if accordingly the meaning is, that God himself then surrounds man like a wall with his
peace, secures his heart and his thoughts, i.e. himself in the core of
his existence—*or* if the peace spoken of is a condition of man, an
added attribute by means of which he can guard himself and so be
secure. But the *en Christō Iēsou* (in Christ Jesus), the addition
'beyond all understanding' and the inversion in v. 9—'the God of
peace'—surely point us most emphatically to the *first* way of
taking it. Not that man is given to understand something, not
that he guards himself by means of a perhaps qualified *nous*
(understanding) of his own, but that he *is* guarded by a peace
which *surpasses* his *nous* or understanding and which is and remains the peace *of God*—*that* is what is said. It is in giving thanks
and *so* bringing your troubles before God, in the act of thanksgiving—for only in that act are you really 'in Christ Jesus'—that
the guarding in question takes place.

And now the remarkable conclusion of this remarkable series:
**Finally, brothers, whatever is true, whatever is honourable,
whatever is righteous, whatever is pure, whatever is kindly,
whatever is praiseworthy, whatever is called a virtue and**

---

[1] The *kai* seems in fact to join v. 7 with v. 6.

deserves recognition—think on that! And what you have learned and received and heard and seen in me—do that! So will the God of peace be with you. What is the point of these verses? It is clear that Paul now, not without a contrast to v. 7, turns from the inmost and loftiest to matters of a most outward and ordinary kind, and seeks to formulate a last direct exhortation. Those, too, who are encircled by the peace of God live in the *world*, and they of all people know it. He would have them know that here there are ordinances and requirements which must at least be thought on, which must be taken account of—*tauta logizesthe* (think on that!). Then, of course over and above that there is something of a special, specifically Christian nature, which (v. 9 is like an arm stretched forward!) has strictly to be *done*—*tauta prassete* (do that!). The *logizesthe* (think on!) of v. 8 naturally must not be contrasted with the *prassete* (do!) in such a way as to suggest that Paul would wish to see only that done which is specified in v. 9, and the other merely thought upon. Yet there is undoubtedly a distinction between the two ideas. V. 8 has often been claimed as a Christian recognition of worldly *culture*. Sure enough, Paul here bids Christians have respect, as in Rom. 13 for the state, so here for everything that is humanly true and good, everything which for any reason and in any way keeps the life also of the *heathen* under control and direction, or is esteemed by them as creative of control and direction. You are to see and recognize it all as a presupposition to which you too are subject. That is the meaning of *logizesthe*. The whole moral world exists as truly as does the natural world, so to speak as its upper half. The Gospel does not overthrow it, does not alter or increase it either, as little as it overthrows, alters or increases the natural order. The world knows very well what is good. Christians are to know it too, no less well than the world but better—that is assuredly the apostle's view. But knowing about the Good is knowledge of God only when the Good is a *commandment* and when the commandment is *kept*. This—the Good as commandment and the keeping of the commandment— is what the Philippians have learned, received and heard and seen from and in Paul. That is what is specifically Christian. That is their existence *en Christō Iēsou* (in Christ Jesus)—do that! Christianity is not ethics, nor does it *have* any special ethic. As Christians, too, we can only think on what everyone has to think on. Christianity is knowledge of God and just for that reason knowing about the *commandments*, being bound to them, and that means (whether man does justice to them or not) *keeping* the commandments. The demand that follows on what we learn and receive from the *apostles*, hear and see in *them*, can never be anything else but: *prassete—do!* Do what *you* are commanded, what you are commanded at this *moment*. What? As soon as you seek to *ask* that, you can only let yourselves be reminded again that you know it well, as all men do. But you are not to ask. You are to *do* what you—else you were not *you*—are *commanded*. The *thanksgiving* of v. 6 and this *doing* will not be things to look for far apart. Hence the same promise here as there (notice the connecting *kai* also in v. 9b!): the God of peace will be with you. He is the God of the *thankful*, the God of the *doers* of the Word.

THE OFFERING WELL PLEASING
TO GOD

4.10–23

But I had great joy in the Lord that your feelings towards me could come to light once more. You had of course long felt that way, but you had no opportunity. Not as if I would complain: for I have learned to accommodate myself to every situation. I can be small, but also great. I have been initiated into each and every condition—to be full and to be hungry, to have abundance and deficiency. I can do everything through him who gives me strength. But it was right of you to share in my distress. You Philippians know indeed yourselves that in the first days of the Gospel, when I set out from Macedonia, no congregation stood to me in a relationship of giving and receiving except you. To Thessalonica, too, you once and a second time sent me something for my needs. It is not the gift I want, but the fruit of it, which turns again to your benefit. I have now all I need, and more. I have become rich through receiving from Epaphroditus your contribution, like a pleasant fragrance, a welcome offering well pleasing to God. My God will satisfy all your needs according to his riches in glory in Christ Jesus. To God our Father be glory for ever and ever. Amen.
Greetings to each of the holy in Christ Jesus. The brothers who are with me send you greetings. All the holy send you greetings, especially those of the imperial court. The grace of the Lord Jesus Christ be with your spirit.

The end of the letter shows us Paul once more, as in 2.14 ff., in concrete action, to a certain extent demonstrating in practice what was said in vv. 8–9. A human picture—but Christian, Pauline humanity. Paul has been given support by the Philippians through their messenger Epaphroditus. The verses 10–20 express his thanks for it. But Paul shows his esteem and appreciation of the gift he has received by *not* using the word 'thanks', by treating it not as a matter of obligation between man and man but as a thing that is great and gratifying because it represents an offering well pleasing to God. The warmth with which Paul says in v. 10: *echarēn megalōs* (had great joy) is no less genuine for that. *Haec vix placuerit Stoico* (a Stoic would surely have found little pleasure in it), says Bengel. But his joy is joy in the spring—the *anathallein, reflorere* (literally 'blossoming' rather than 'coming to light' of the Philippians' feelings, v. 10), which he sees bestowed on the readers in the fact that they found opportunity, by helping *him*, to make an offering to God (v. 18). It was not *his* needs they helped, he says in vv. 11-17. Not, of course, because he has not suffered need. But he has long learned to accommodate himself to any situation. Not through heroism on his own part, is again a necessary reservation: *emathon* (I have *learned*) in v. 11, *oida* (I can, strictly 'I know how to') and *memuēmai* (I have been initiated) in v. 12—all these expressions imply: I do not have it from myself. And v. 13 confirms that: I can do everything through him who *makes* me strong. He has, as the *memuēmai* in v. 12 significantly says, 'initiated' him—namely, into the mystery of life with its ups and downs of having and being without. Well then—it was not his needs that they helped. Needs there were. But they were otherwise remedied—namely, through him who made him strong to be able for everything, able to endure. Nevertheless (v. 14) they did well with their active participation.

In vv. 15 ff. Paul makes another new start: it is not the case either that the Philippians' gift is in accordance with some regular relationship between the apostle and his congregations. What has happened here is an exception. He does not rejoice in the gift, nor even, as we could now expect, in the human givers, but in the *fruit*, his further work which is made possible by the gift, and which will also be to the benefit of the givers (v. 17). He feels himself enriched through the gift because he knows it is an *offering* made to God and well pleasing to God (v. 18). The man who in 2.17 conceived of himself—of the surrender of his life—as a libation, may well speak thus. He may thank without thanking, by pointing to his God who in his glory will be mindful also of their needs (v. 19). So the letter ends with the same objectivity and superiority with which it began, and in which it is at once both one of the most remarkable evidences of how human a Christian can be *and* a testimony to an event which can only be designated as the very *limit* of what is understood by human history.

BIBLIOGRAPHY

Chrysostom, *Homilies on the Epistle to the Philippians.*

Zwingli, *In epistolam ad Philippenses annotationes* (Works, ed. M. Schuler and J. Schulthess, VI, 2).

Luther, *Works,* Erlangen Edition.

Calvin, *Commentarius in epistolam ad Philippenses* (Corp. Ref. Op. Calv. vol. 52) 1548.

Bengel, *Gnomon Novi Testamenti* tom. II, 1742.

C. H. Rieger, *Betrachtungen über das N. T.,* 3. Teil, 1828.

J. Chr. K. v. Hofmann, *Die heil. Schrift N.T'es,* 4. Teil, 3. Abt., 1871.

H. A. W. Meyer, *Krit. Exeget. Kommentar über das NT,* 9. Abt. 2. Aufl. 1859, 8. Aufl. by Ernst Lohmeyer, 1927.

W. Lueken, *Der Brief an die Philipper* (in Joh. Weiss, *Die Schriften des NT*), 1906.

M. Dibelius, *An die Philipper* (in Lietzmann, *Handbuch zum NT*), 1913.

A. Schlatter, *Erläuterungen zum NT,* Band II, 1923.

Ewald-Wohlenberg, *Der Brief des Paulus an die Philipper* (in Zahn, *Kommentar zum NT*), 3. Aufl. 1923.

Fritz Horn, *Die Scheidung der Geister (Der Brief des Jakobus und der Brief des Paulus an die Philipper),* Worms and Lüthgen in Crefeld, undated.